Is your brain COLOSSAL? ☐
Have you got FOUR feet? ☐
Would you like to be a MUMMY? ☐
And have BICYCLES to EAT? ☐

Have you tasted CHÂTEAU PIDDLE? ☐
Have you seen it raining FROGS? ☐
Have you gone shopping on a LLAMA? ☐
Have you met the world's MOST FAITHFUL DOGS? ☐

Answers

8 ✓ : Hm. You *could* be the World's Worst Liar. For other
World's Worsts, see pages 29–30.

4–7 ✓ : You're probably weird enough to get into the
Weird Records.

0–3 ✓ : You could be normal – it's just possible. This book
is for you.

0 ✓ and 0 ✗ : No pen or pencil? You need one too big to
lose. See page 70.

# CUNNINGHAM'S LITTLE RED RECORD BOOK

### BRONNIE CUNNINGHAM

*Illustrated by*
*Rowan Barnes-Murphy*

**PUFFIN BOOKS**

Puffin Books, Penguin Books Ltd, Harmondsworth, Middlesex, England
Penguin Books, 625 Madison Avenue, New York, New York 10022, U.S.A.
Penguin Books Australia Ltd, Ringwood, Victoria, Australia
Penguin Books Canada Ltd, 2801 John Street, Markham, Ontario, Canada L3R 1B4
Penguin Books (N.Z.) Ltd, 182–190 Wairau Road, Auckland 10, New Zealand

—

First published 1981

—

—

Made and printed in Great Britain by
Richard Clay (The Chaucer Press) Ltd.
Bungay, Suffolk
Set in Monotype Baskerville

# CONTENTS

**Acknowledgements** 1

**Weird Records** 9

*stinkers; dirty kings; kissing; wacky races; spittin', belchin' and cussin'; ugliest face; odd jobs; weird, weirder and weirdest records; all-white picture; world's worst.*

**Money Marvels** 31

*one million records; richest people; luckiest gamblers; most expensive shopping list; Christmas presents; stamps.*

**Particular and Peculiar Places** 43

*countries; islands; strange places; froggy showers; houses; the world's worst spelling mistake.*

**Space and Spirits** 56

*into space; space animals; U.F.O.s; ghosts.*

**Mostest** 64

*biggest; biggest chocolate factories; smallest; fastest; collections; record records; motorcycles.*

**Endurance and Survival** 86

*long-distance and endurance records; strong men and women; survivors; desert island records.*

**Stunts and Other Lunacies** 89

*daredevils and barnstormers; Niagara walkers; live mummies.*

**Fun and Games**  105

*Olympic records; football; curious cricket; Monopoly; chess; games; teddy bears and dolls.*

**Amazing Animals**  123

*cats; dogs; most faithful dogs; remote-control collies; horses; dinosaurs; most venomous; mysterious footprints; mummies.*

**Kids**  141

*youngest; wildest; prodigies; mathematical whizz-kids; record-making; twins; schools.*

**Freaky Families**  157

*parents; babies; weddings; nutty names.*

**Batty Bodies**  166

*batty bits; death-defying bodies.*

**Food**  176

*fantastic; parties, feasts and banquets; revolting food; most disgusting and most delicious; drink; swallowing; amazing half-eaten-apple clue; weirdest places to eat.*

**The Missing Record**  191

# ACKNOWLEDGEMENTS

I would like to thank all the very many people who gave me expert advice and generous help, particularly: Carol A. R. Andrews of the British Museum; Marvin Berglas; Lew Cady; Peter Eldin, Michael Colley and John Salisse of the Magic Circle; I. D. D. Eaves of H.M. Tower of London; Margaret Turfrey of the Publishers' Association; Pam Goodger, P.R.O. at Longleat House; Col. Robert Henderson; Roy W. Pratt; Brian Rust; Mr and Mrs David Pritchard; Joan Palmer, editor of *Dog News*; Jon Wynne-Tyson; R. F. Scales of Waddingtons; The Hershey Foods Corporation, Pennsylvania; The Football Association; C. J. Freezer, editor of *Model Railways*; Mrs D. Allan of Hamleys Ltd; the editorial staff of *Motorcycling Monthly*, *Stamp Monthly* and *Scouting Magazine*; the B.T.A. Information Library, London, NW1; and especially Patrick Cunningham.

Dear Reader,

The author would be very grateful if you would take care of the records in this book.

Please do not break or smash them.

Thank you.

*Bronnie Cunningham*

# Weird Records

### STINKERS

**Most powerful.** The world's most powerful pong is
4-hydroxy-3-methoxy-benzaldehyde. If you put a roof
over a football pitch and sat on a beam 14 m (45 ft
11 ins.) up in the roof, and if someone way down below
you let one tiny drop of the stuff escape, you could
still get a whiff of it. (Unless you had a cold, of course.)

9

**World's worst.** Of all the 17,000 different smells which have been identified, including smelly socks, possibly the world's worst is ethyl mercaptan (CHSH). That smells like rotten slimy cabbages, plus a powerful stink of garlic, mixed with the odour of old lavatories.

**Best smeller.** A male silk-worm moth can smell a female silk-worm moth 10·6 km (6·8 miles) away.

**Art.** Dieter Rot held an exhibition of cheese art in Los Angeles, California, U.S.A., consisting of forty suit-cases, filled with more than a ton of different cheeses, packed into the pockets and pouches in forty-eight different ways. The exhibition was due to last for a month. The artist left after four days, by which time there was such a rare, rich and revolting aroma arising from the rotting cheese that he feared the police would close the exhibition. They did.

**Smell-making factory.** International Flavors and Fragrances, Inc., of New York are the world's biggest makers of smells and tastes. With hundreds of chemicals they can make strawberry and beefburger tastes, or the smell of coffee, or even rancid water-buffalo butter.

**The smelliest bath.** Cecil B. de Mille made a film in 1932 about the Roman Empress Poppaea, who used to bath every day in asses' milk. So he got a huge bath, filled it with four hundred gallons of real milk, with blobs of lard floating on the top to look like cream. The scene took a week to film. The hot studio lights shone down. By the end of the week, the star, Claudette

Colbert, was bathing in a slimy, cheesy, almost solid, stinking bath. After filming, the bath was left overnight, and the floating fats set on top. Next day, a publicity man, showing visitors over the set, thought it was a marble floor, stepped on to it, and disappeared from sight. When he came up he was *not* a pretty sight, *nor* a pretty smell.

**The real stinker.** Andrew Smullian was hired by a firm in 1979 as a stinking debt-collector. His job was to visit firms that owed money, smelling so disgusting that they would pay up to get him to leave. It worked very well. He dressed in foul tramp's clothes, sewed rotten fish into the lining of the coat, and sprayed himself with a stinking compost formula made by his old school chemistry master. The filthy pong carried 65 yds down the road. In an office, it was overpowering. He never had to sit there more than half an hour. A few whiffs of Smelly Smullian made them pay up at once. Smullian has permanently blocked sinuses, and his girl friends 'come and go'.

# DIRTY KINGS
## AND OTHER WASHING RECORDS

**Royalty.** King John took a bath *once every three weeks*.

Queen Elizabeth had a bath *once a month* – and she was considered *very clean*.

King Louis XIV of France bathed *once a year*.

King Frederick the Great of Prussia *hardly ever even washed his face*.

King Louis XIII of France had only had five baths in his life, when he became King at the age of 10 – and after his fifth bath he was sent back to bed for the whole day to recover!

**Democracy.** In 1840 the people of Pennsylvania, U.S.A., tried to get a law passed to *stop anyone having a bath between November and March*. They sewed their children into long winter underwear in the autumn and undid them in the spring.

**Biggest bath.** King George IV had a marble bathtub made for the Royal Pavilion at Brighton 16 ft long, 10 ft wide and 6 ft deep – a king-size bath.

**Cold baths.** Children in the 19th century were allowed one *warm* bath a week. Every morning they stood in the bathtub, and cold water was poured over them, slowly, for 2 mins.

**Fruitiest bath.** Whenever fresh fruit was available, Madame Tallien, a lady at the court of Louis XIV in France, took a bath in crushed strawberries.

**Once a year.** Every citizen of the state of Kentucky, U.S.A., is required by law to take a bath once a year.

(And, for *your own bath record* – see Personal Record inside the front cover.)

# KISSING, APPLE-PEELING
## AND OTHER PASTIMES

**Kissing.** On St Valentine's Day, 14 February 1978, in Florida, U.S.A., Debbie Luray and Jim Schuyler began kissing the *world's longest kiss* – for charity, so they said. It lasted 5 days 12 hrs (with some rest intervals to get up steam again)!

James Whale of Metro Radio, Newcastle upon Tyne, kissed 4,049 willing girls in 8 glorious hours on 22 September 1978. It wasn't for charity, and it can't have been for love – not 4,049 girls, surely – so it must have been to set a record.

(If these records have been broken, don't blame me. People *will* keep breaking them. Kissing records are very popular – I can't think why.)

**Joking.** G. David Howard cracked jokes for 16 hrs in July 1979 at Clearwater Beach, Florida, U.S.A. There's no record of anyone actually laughing at them.

**Yarn-spinning.** Frank Hardy is the Yarn Spinning Champion of Australia. He defeated the champion, Tall-Tale Tex, who had beaten the notorious Walkie-Talkie-Walker. It happened in Darwin, Australia. Frank Hardy's hobby was collecting Australian folk stories, and he'd invented quite a few too. Tall-Tale Tex heard Hardy was in town and threw out a challenge. The yarn-spinning went on for $11\frac{1}{2}$ hrs. They closed the shops and relayed the tales outside on loudspeakers. Eventually Hardy saw a blank look come across Tall-Tale Tex's face, and he knew he'd won.

**House-breaking.** Thirteen muscle men from the East Anglian Martial Arts Club kicked and punched and demolished a three-bedroomed house in King's Lynn, Norfolk, on 19 August 1979. In 61 mins. they brought down 7,000 bricks and eleven doors.

**Car-cramming.** Seventy-three Scouts and Cubs from Leckhampton, Cheltenham, crammed themselves into and on to a Mini on 24 June 1979.

One hundred and eleven members of Glendale Secondary School, Hamilton, Ontario, Canada, piled into and on top of a stationary Volkswagen in November 1969, but the car couldn't be driven.

**Slow-bicycling.** David Steel of Tucson, Arizona, U.S.A., stayed stationary without support on a bicycle for 9 hrs 15 mins. on 25 November 1977. (That was a Friday – maybe he'd sat on an office chair all Thursday, and wanted a change.)

**Apple-peeling.**
The longest unbroken apple peel cut from one apple, weighing 567 g (20 oz.), is 172 ft 2 ins. (52·5 m). Katy Wafler, aged 17, of Wolcott, New York, U.S.A., took 11 hrs 30 mins. to do it in October 1976.

# WACKY RACES AND OTHER
# CRAZY COMPETITIONS

**Baths.** The annual International Bath Tub Race is held over a 36-mile course near Vancouver, British Columbia. The baths are fitted with 6-h.p. engines, and must not exceed 1·90 m in length. Record time: 1 hr 29 mins. 40 secs. Record distance achieved by a *hand-propelled* bathtub is 36·6 miles (58·9 km) in 24 hrs.

**Spitting.** The annual tobacco-spitting contest is held at Raleigh, Mississippi, U.S.A. Record-holder is Don Snyder with 31 ft 1 in. (9·47 m). Prizes are given for furthest, most accurate and most compact.

**Woggle-hopping.** Woggle-hopping is the invention of George Corner and means leap-frogging over letter-boxes. He has his own letter-box on the front lawn in Woodkirk, Yorkshire. He made a tour of England, taking a running jump over 1,000 letter-boxes on the way.

**Farts.** Many towns in ancient Japan held farting contests. S.B.D.s – silent but deadly – never won. The prizes went to the loudest and longest, and the winners were held in great honour.

**Snail's pace race.** The Fifth International Snail-racing Championships were won by the favourite in Murillo de Rio Leza, Spain, in 1979. His name was Pepe, and he was a really fast-moving snail, beating 200 rivals from Europe and South America, covering the 4 ft 8 in. (1·4 m) course in well under the 6-min. limit.

**Pancakes.** The oldest and most famous pancake race takes place on Shrove Tuesday at Olney, Bucks. Housewives set off from the church when the pancake bell is rung, tossing their pancakes three times on the way. The winner gets a kiss from the verger and a prayer book from the vicar. The distance is 415 yds (380 m) and the record time 61·0 secs.

**Eggmobiles.** In the Great Egg Race held in London in 1980 the idea was to move an egg 12 m in the fastest possible time, with the help of a single elastic band. 500 eggmobiles entered. Lionel Reyes's model 'Oeuf and Puff', weighing just over a third of an ounce and made of aluminium tubing braced with steel wire 1/10,000 in. thick, covered 12 m in 4·09 secs. No one has yet broken the 4-sec. barrier. (Experts believe the fastest speed possible over 12 m is 12 m.p.h. or 19·3 km/h.)

**Custard pies.** The World Custard Pie Championships are held each year at Coxheath, Kent. Each team has four members, and in the final they each throw ten pies at their opponent, 2·53 m (8 ft 4 ins.) away. Scoring: 6 points for a direct hit, full in face; 3 points for a near miss, shoulder upwards; 1 point for a body hit. Real custard ricochets, so the pies are flour and water paste in a real pastry case. Most frequent winners: The Birds and the Coxheath Man.

## SPITTIN', BELCHIN' AND CUSSIN' TRIATHLON

This competition takes place in Central City, Colorado, U.S.A., on 1 April.

**Belching.** Each entrant has 30 secs. to submit his or her entry. (And one more try after that.) The judges are three members of the Denver Symphony Orchestra, who look out for good tone, as well as loud volume. The most recent champion was Chris Gossett, aged 21, who belched out a version of 'Hello, Dolly'. He got a huge can of beans for winning, and gave it to the runner-up, Miss Terri Fleming, aged 15.

**Cussing and swearing.** This competition is open to all ages, but some children find it difficult to get their parents' permission to enter. The cusser has 1 min. for cussing. A victim is provided, to be cussed at – usually a politician, but once it was a minister. Best scores go for originality. The most recent winner called himself

David DeGross, but his real name was Dave Nolan. His prize was a case of Ivory Soap. We understand the winning entry went something like this ... (unprintable – sorry.)

**Spitting.** The rules forbid use of watermelon seeds, stones or any other aid – just natural juices. Judges are posted downrange to follow the airborne flight to its final resting place. Nothing smaller than a dime is counted – no sprays, definitely. Most recent winner was Earl 'The Squirrel', winning with a distance of 32 ft 7 ins. (9·92 m). Prize: a spittoon. The *world record* for spitting was reached in this competition in 1973 – 34 ft $\frac{1}{4}$ in. (10·36 m) by Harold Fielden.

## THE UGLIEST FACE IN THE WORLD

The World Gurning Championships are held in September every year, at Egremont, Cumbria, England,

to find the man or woman who can pull the world's worst, most horrible and awful face.

The Championships are part of the annual Crab Fair and take place in the evening. Each competitor puts his (or her) head through a *braffin,* which is a great big leather horse's collar. Then he puts on the most frightful expression he can, puffing and blowing his cheeks, rolling the eyes, going all cross-eyed, screwing his lower lip up to his nose and looking as loony as he can. (The winner in 1978–9 was, in fact, Mr Ron Looney.)

There is also a Junior Section – for the Ugliest Young Mug in the World. (Won by Tom Mattinson of Aspatria in 1978 and 1979.)

## ODD JOBS

**Professional nail-biters.** The *ramanga*, a group of servants in Madagascar in the 18th century, had the job of eating all the nail pairings and blood lost by members of the upper classes. If the nails were too long or jagged, they were minced first. If a noble cut himself, the ramanga licked his wounds. If a nail broke, or blood flowed when the ramanga wasn't there, the noble would nobly save them for him.

**Dice-swallowers.** In English gambling dens in the 18th century, a man was employed whose only job was to swallow the dice if the place was raided.

**Ghost-train tickler.** The last recorded ghost-train

tickler died in Sussex in 1970. His job was to hide up in the darkness and scare the passengers by tickling them with a long feather.

**The Council fool.** Crewe Council hired Michael Hirst for a fortnight in the summer of 1978 as a council fool. He was provided with a jester costume, cap and bells to amuse and tickle the shoppers. A council spokesman said: 'Michael is just the fool we're looking for.'

**Human organ.** The human organ was invented by J. A. Maresch in 1751 in Russia. The instrument consisted of forty horns, each one blown by a serf, whose whole life was spent blowing just one note. This must be the most boring job ever recorded. Human organs were tremendously popular and nobles bought and sold entire organ teams.

**Chicken-hatcher.** The only human chicken-hatcher on record is a French soldier in Napoleon's army, called Savan. Savan deserted in Egypt, was captured and ordered to do heavy duty. Savan refused – and when they asked why, he said he was really too weak to do anything but sit around.

So they gave him a job just sitting around. A nest of hen's eggs was prepared and Savan was placed on it – and kept sitting until he had hatched out three broods of chickens.

## WEIRD RECORDS

**Snakiest lavatory.** On 31 October 1978 Mr Lennart Persson of Göteborg, Sweden, found a 4-ft boa constrictor in his lavatory pan.

**The fishiest cheque.** On 17 January 1980 James Sullivan, a Cornish fishmonger, wrote out a cheque for £222 71p on the belly of an 8 ft 350 lb. shark. (The cheque was for the Council, to pay his rates, which he thought were unfair.) He handed the shark-cheque over to the Council; the Council took the shark-cheque to the Midland Bank and they paid out the money.

**Allergy.** The most extraordinary allergy on record is of a man allergic to the number eighteen. The very thought of it made him feel sick and giddy.

**Shut-eye.** Herr Heinrich Laufer of Germany holds the record for keeping one eye shut for ninety days. Herr Laufer was discovered spying on his landlord's wife. The landlord threatened to bring the law on him, but Laufer confessed to a priest, who ordered him – as a penance – to keep his wicked eye shut for three months. The landlord kept *his* eye on *him* to make sure he did.

**Quietest guest.** José Luis Huenchupa was the quietest guest at a very noisy three-day party held near Santiago, Chile, in May 1978. The noise didn't worry him, though. He died on the first day and no one noticed.

**Own jail.** Semsettin Semsettin, a prisoner serving an eighteen-month sentence in a jail in Incesu, Kayseri, Turkey, bought the jail in January 1980. 'Now I feel really at home,' he said.

**Road sign.** A small town in Pennsylvania, U.S.A., could never get motorists to slow down as they went through. No warning signs or notices begging them to go slowly would work, until they put up the world's most efficient road sign –

CAUTION – NUDISTS CROSSING

## WEIRDER RECORDS

**Deadliest throne.** Emperor Menelik II of Abyssinia ordered three American electric chairs – a new invention – for his country in 1890. When they arrived, there was a slight hitch. Emperor Menelik had forgotten that Abyssinia had no electricity. So he used one as his Imperial Throne.

**Coffin car.** Mrs Sandra West, aged 37, a Texan millionairess, was buried in a lace night-gown in her favourite Ferrari car, in accordance with her last wish.

**Alsatian sweater.** Mrs Lesley Corbett-Wilson of Bosham, Sussex, is the only recorded owner of an alsatian sweater. She spent four years collecting the moulting hair of her dog, Viva, and then spun it and knitted it into a black, cream and fawn sweater.

**Eggiest jam.** The eggiest traffic jam happened in the Tokyo suburb of Suginami in the morning rush hour on 5 October 1977. A lorry carrying 66,000 eggs turned over; traffic was held up for 3 hrs while two fire-engines poured sand on to the *world's biggest uncooked scrambled egg*.

**Eggiest bridge.** A bridge in Lima, Peru, called the Bridge of Eggs was built with mortar mixed with the whites of 10,000 eggs instead of water.

**Drunkest fish.** The tipsiest fish in the world is the first fish caught each season at St Malo, Normandy, France. The fisherman pours half a bottle of wine down its throat and throws it back, to encourage the other fish to come and be caught.

**Keenest bookworm.** Gustave Leban went to the Bibliothèque Nationale in Paris every day for sixty years to read the same book – 'St Apolonius of Tiane'.

**Billiards.** An American called Henry Lewis made a break of 46 at billiards, *with his nose*.

**Incredible exports.** The Premier Drum Company of Leicester won the Incredible Export Award for exporting maracas to Caracas, bongos to the Congo and sleigh-bells to Lapland.

A Dutch company sold 5 tonnes of sand to Saudi Arabia. (For filtering their swimming-pool water.)

A Danish firm shipped 50,000 do-it-yourself ice-lollies to Greenland. The Eskimoes can just leave them out of doors most of the year to freeze.

British firms have sold: chow mein to Hong Kong, sun-lamps to Australia, artificial sponges to Tahiti and lions all round the world.

**Deadest king.** King Kokodo of the Congo is the only king known to have ruled for three years after his death. His body was moved around in a square coffin on wheels, and he was supplied with food and money while he made up his mind whether to stay dead or not. He decided to stay dead.

**Dear Departed.** When Mr Van Butchell's wife died in 1775, he had her embalmed and dressed in a fine linen gown. He put her in a glass-topped case and kept her in the drawing-room. When visitors came, he introduced her as 'My Dear Departed' and she was very popular. So many people came to meet her that he had to say: No Visitors on Sunday. But when he married again, his second wife got a bit fed up with her standing around all the time, so the Dear Departed was removed to the Royal College of Surgeons in London. A bomb finally blew her to heaven in May 1941.

**Parrot funeral.** The grandest parrot funeral on record is the funeral of His Most Gracious Majesty the Lord Grimsby of Katmandu – a parrot – owned by David Bates of Preston, Lancashire.

Lord Grimsby lay in state on a silken bed for three weeks; his casket was covered with 1,000 carnations; he had a diamond ring on his beak and a little crown on his head, and he was surrounded by palm leaves and candles in silver candelabra. Solemn poetry was recited over his little crowned head.

**Pack of cards.** Frank Damek of Chicago, Illinois, U.S.A., compiled a complete pack of cards by picking them up one at a time off the street. After ten years he was still fifteen cards short and it took him another twenty years to pick up the missing ones.

**Smartest snowmen.** Madame de la Bresse of Paris left 125,000 francs to provide snowmen with clothes. The will was contested in court – and the snowmen won.

**Best-dressed goldfish.** Francesca Nortyuege of Dieppe, France, left her fortune to her niece on condition that, for the sake of decency, she kept her goldfish clothed in little body-stockings.

# THE WORLD'S FIRST
# ALL-WHITE PICTURE

Alphonse Allais showed a painting in a Paris exhibition
in 1883 called

    'First Communion of Anaemic Young Girls
        in the Snow'.

It was 26·5 cm × 35 cm (10·3 ins. × 13·8 ins.) and
looked like this. (The four things in the corners are
drawing-pins.)

It was just a sheet of white Bristol paper, with nothing
on it whatsoever.

Next year he showed an ALL RED picture, which we
can't show you because we haven't any red, called
'Apoplectic Cardinals Harvesting Tomatoes on the
Shore of the Red Sea'. This was a sheet of *red* Bristol
paper, with nothing on it whatsoever.

# THE WORLD'S WORST

**Hiccupers.** Jack O'Leary of Los Angeles hiccuped 160 million times between 1948 and 1956. He tried 60,000 cures. Finally, he sent up a prayer to St Jude, patron saint of lost causes – and recovered.

Charles Osborne of Anthon, Iowa, started hiccuping in 1922 and he's *still doing it.*

**Home-coming.** Mr Bail of 41 Victoria Street, Flixton, Lancashire, went on holiday in June 1978. While he was away, the demolition men came to knock down No. 43. Mr Bail came home on 30 June to find there had been a slight mistake. They had knocked down No. 41 instead of No. 43.

**Orchestra.** Martin Lewis, manager and record producer of the Portsmouth Sinfonia Orchestra, is quite, absolutely and altogether sure that his orchestra is the worst in the world. (That's not counting any perfectly awful school orchestra you may have heard – because people don't actually pay to hear them!)

**Most boring book.** An American survey names *The Pilgrim's Progress* by John Bunyan as the most boring classic book ever written. (I don't agree, do you? See Personal Record inside the front cover.)

**Worst fears.** Another American poll asked 3,000 Americans, 'What are you most afraid of?' The first three at the top of the list were:

1. Speaking in front of a group of people: 41 per cent
2. Heights: 32 per cent
3. Insects and bugs: 22 per cent.

**Golfer.** A woman golfer took 166 shots at the 16th hole in a Ladies International match at Shawnee-on-Delaware, in Pennsylvania, U.S.A. First, she hit a screwy drive and the ball splashed into the Binniekill River. She and her husband got into a boat and went after it. He rowed and she flailed away at the ball. By the time she hit it out, they were $1\frac{1}{2}$ miles downstream. Then she hacked it back through the woods towards the green, sinking it on the 166th stroke. Every shot was carefully recorded by her husband – the rat!

**Sneezer.** Tricia Reay, aged 12, of Sutton Coldfield, broke the world sneezing record on 18 March 1980. The previous record was 155 days, set by an American girl, but 18 March was Tricia's 156th sneezing day – and still she went on sneezing and sneezing. They hypnotized her. They anaesthetized her nose. They tried a hundred and one different cures. Nothing worked. Aaaa . . . tish . . . shoo, all day long. She finally stopped on 25 April, after 194 days.

# Money Marvels

## ONE MILLION RECORDS

**£1,000,000 notes.** Two Bank of England £1 million notes still exist. They were printed before 1812, and £1 million then would be worth at least £20 million now, so that's a mighty big note to have in your wallet or purse. They were used *inside* the Bank and *not* handed out over the counter.

**$1,000,000 bank error.** The Mellon Bank of Pittsburgh, Pennsylvania, made a big mistake in July 1978. They put $1 million into the bank account of Mr Melchor Javier and his wife Victoria of Manila in the Philippine Islands, instead of $1,000. Mr and Mrs Javier were very pleased to get the money and started spending it and putting it into other banks right away. The Mellon Bank are trying to get their $999,000 back.

**£1,000,000 reward.** The biggest prize ever offered – £1 million – is waiting for the person who can hand over: ' A device which can be proved to have been activated to arrive on earth from beyond our solar system. Such a device must be either: a craft capable of interstellar travel which has transported extra-terrestrial beings to earth; or an unmanned reconnaissance vehicle; or a missile; or an artifact.'

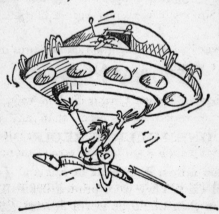

In other words, if you can find a U.F.O. from outer space – you win £1 million. (Reward offered by a British whisky firm in 1979.)

**£1,000,000 footballer.** Trevor Francis became Britain's first million-pound footballer when Nottingham Forest paid Birmingham City a £1 million transfer fee for him on 4 February 1979.

## THE RICHEST PEOPLE
## IN THE WORLD

**Dollar billionaires.** The only billionaire alive now is Mr Daniel K. Ludwig of Michigan, U.S.A., who is estimated to be worth $3 billion. (A billion dollars is $1,000 million, or about £500 million.) Mr Ludwig owns a great deal of property and the world's third largest tanker fleet. He started in business when he was 9 years old. That's when he bought his first boat. It was sunk at the time, but it only cost $25, and judging from his later success it must have been a bargain.

Just over half of the 250,000 millionaires in America today are women.

**The Amir of Kuwait,** who died in 1965, probably made more money every week than any man ever known. His huge income came from royalties on oil. Every week he got £2·6 million pocket money.

**The richest man in Britain** is thought to be John Moores, who was born in Eccles, Lancashire, and left school in 1910 when he was 14 years old. (The school-leaving age was lower in those days.) His first job was as a telephone operator, and thirteen years later he founded

Littlewoods football pools. In 1979 he was worth about £850 million, give or take a million or two.

**The Nizam of Hyderabad,** an Indian Prince who ruled over a state the size of Germany and who died in 1966, was the world's richest man and left behind him probably the world's most valuable collection of gold and jewels. To this day no one knows for sure how large the treasure is.

The Nizam had many magnificent palaces, and their subterranean passages were stuffed with gold blocks laden on trucks, barrels of emeralds, diamonds and rubies, including one walnut-sized 180-carat diamond, crates of black pearls, a solid gold 150-piece dinner service, jade carvings, porcelain, furniture, and precious carpets which had never even been unrolled. His jewels alone were thought to be worth £400 million.

The Nizam ordered Rolls-Royces by the dozen, all numbered Kothi 123. (King Kothi Palace was one of his mansions.) In the two World Wars he gave the British two corvettes, a squadron of Spitfires and about £8 million. But he himself lived an almost frugal life, despite being surrounded by thousands of retainers. He was a scholar and poet, and a bit of a miser. A visitor who went to tea with him noticed that his clothes had been most carefully darned.

## THE LUCKIEST GAMBLERS

**The biggest lottery.** Spain's Christmas lottery is called *El Gordo*, the Fat One, and it pays out more prize money than any other lottery in the world. In December 1979, during its centenary year, the Fat One was the Fattest ever – paying out over £200 million. £40 million of this went to the members of one church in a small town called Branollers. Father Samper, the parish priest, had sold tickets at 65p each, on condition that one quarter of the winnings would go to mend the church roof. For each ticket the winner got £5,517. Father Samper won more than £55,000 and the church won £10 million.

**The world's most cautious gambler.** In 1950 at the Las Vegas Desert Inn in Nevada, U.S.A., an anonymous sailor made a record twenty-seven straight wins with the dice at a crap game. (The odds against this are 12,467,890 to 1.) If he had bet as much as he was allowed to on each throw, he would have won $268 million. But he didn't. Maybe he just couldn't believe in his luck? Anyway, his bets were so small that he only won $750. The Las Vegas Desert Inn were so astounded and relieved that they have kept the dice ever since, under glass and on a velvet pillow.

**Biggest single win.** Miron Vieira de Sousa of Brazil won £1,065,891 for a 25p bet on the Brazilian football pools in 1975. The first thing he did? He went out and bought himself a set of false teeth!

David Preston of Burton-on-Trent won a total £953,874 10p on Littlewoods and Vernon Pools in February 1980, a British record. The following week he tried his luck again – and increased his winnings by almost £1!

# THE WORLD'S MOST EXPENSIVE SHOPPING LIST

**1½lb. tomatoes – £200** (A Dublin restaurant paid that price for seven Irish Republic tomatoes on 31 January 1980.)

**A bottle of wine – $14,000** (An American paid that price for a bottle of 1806 Château Lafite-Rothschild – the most expensive bottle of wine in the world.)

**One sandwich – £20** (A woman called Fanny Murray clapped a £20 note between two slices of bread and butter and ate it. That was a long time ago. By now, that £20 would be worth £200 – some sandwich!)

**One banana – £3,000** (Lord Leconfield of Petworth, Sussex, was told by a friend that bananas tasted best when picked straight from the plant. So he spent £3,000 growing his own bananas. The butler brought the first one to him on a golden dish. He cut a slice with a golden knife, put it in his mouth with a golden fork, said: 'Oh God, it tastes like any other damned banana' and threw it away. So that's £3,000 for *one slice*. He never bothered to eat another home-grown banana.)

**One Easter egg** – £125,000 (The price paid in an auction for an egg given to the Tsarina of Russia by her husband, Nicholas II. Made by Fabergé in gold and precious stones, it opens to reveal a statue of the Tsar on his horse.)

**One watch** – £45,000 (Cost of the most expensive man's standard pocket watch you can buy anywhere – the Swiss *Grande Complication* by Ardemars Piguet.)

**One pair of shoes** – £3,575 (Mink-lined golf shoes, with gold trimmings and ruby spikes, made in Northampton, England.)

**A licence plate for the car** – $35,000 (Cost of the first plate, A1 – bought by an American collector in 1973.)

**A paper table napkin** – £500 (Cost of a paper table napkin from the Las Vegas Riviera Hotel, Nevada, signed and inscribed by Elvis Presley. Bought by the owner of a pub in Covent Garden, London, at an auction on 3 March 1980.)

**Toy** – £3,000 (The most expensive toy ever sold at Hamleys of Regent Street, London – the world's biggest toy shop – was a little steam traction engine, only 12 ins. high and 14 ins. long which could pull a full-size motor-car.)

## THE WORLD'S MOST UNUSUAL AND EXPENSIVE CHRISTMAS PRESENTS

In 1976 the Sakowitz department store in Texas, U.S.A., offered for sale some 'Ultimate Gifts', including:

One night learning to pole-slide and being a fireman – £125

A part in an M.G.M. movie – £1,250

The chance to conduct the Houston Symphony Orchestra for one performance – £7,250 (Bought by a Florida grandmother for her grandson.)

A French château in the Sauternes district, with sixty acres of vines – £435,000

The chance to invent your own original ice-cream flavour, plus 100 gallons of the ice-cream – £375

Make a record with a rock group – £3,500

A Caribbean island of 63 acres – £1,125,000

An all-day photographic session for a centre-page picture in *Playboy* magazine – the nude page – £250.

The person who was given the present acted as the nude model (Four of these were sold.)

AND – THE ultimate gift – One bathtub and the diamonds in said bathtub that it would take to cover an average female adult up to the neck – £59 million

## STAMPS

**Penny Blacks.** The British penny black stamp – first issued on 6 May 1840 – was the world's first adhesive postage stamp. Sixty-eight million were issued, so a used and slightly damaged copy will not be worth a great deal. However, an unused penny black can be worth £2,500. Also very valuable is a cover stamped with any May date.

**Twopenny Blues.** Twopenny blue stamps were issued two days later than the penny blacks. Only six million were printed. A perfect example can fetch £5,000.

**Penny Reds.** Penny red stamps were first issued in 1841. Later issues of this stamp have numbers in all four corners, with the plate number printed down both sides of the stamp. The rarest plate – worth thousands of pounds – is Plate No. 77.

**The first real British postage stamp** was a triangular handstamp saying 'Penny Post Paid', used from 1680 to 1682. The postal service was run by William Dockwra in London and Westminster.

**The most valuable collection of British and Commonwealth stamps** belongs to the Queen. She has a Keeper to look after her collection of 350 albums. The Queen doesn't have to put her own stamp on her letters and she doesn't have to lick the back of her head and stick her face on to envelopes. All Royal letters are stamped with a special Royal postmark.

**The most expensive stamp ever issued in Great Britain** is the Victorian £5 stamp, issued in 1882.

**The world's most valuable stamp.** Only one copy of the British Guiana 1 cent black and magenta 1856 stamp exists in the world today. It was discovered in 1873 by a 12-year-old English schoolboy, Vernon Vaughan, living in Georgetown in British Guiana. He wanted to buy some other stamps, so he sold it to a Scotsman for $1½ (about 30p).

Five years later the Scotsman sold it to a Frenchman for £150. Arthur Hind, a Texas oil millionaire, paid £7,000 for it in Paris in 1922 and kept it until he died in 1933, but a strange thing is said to have happened in 1929. Someone offered Mr Hind *another* stamp, exactly the same as his, for £20,000. Mr Hind, it is said, bought it and set fire to it, so that his stamp would be the only one in the world. On 5 April 1980 this one stamp was auctioned in New York and fetched $850,000. A lot of people, including stamp dealers, are scouring attics in Guiana, just in case there's an old 1856 envelope hiding somewhere.

**Curiosities.** The country of Tonga once issued a stamp shaped like a banana.

Albania issued a stamp to commemorate the world's heaviest smoker. Ahmed Zogu smoked an average of 240 cigarettes a day – but not for long.

Many stamps have been wrongly printed, with missing colours, overprinting or parts of the design left out, but the most startling example was the 'Opening of the Post Office Tower' stamp, issued on 8 October 1965, cost 3d. The picture of the Post Office Tower itself is missing!

In 1965 a Scottish schoolboy bought a stamp for 6d. (3p) and sold it at auction for £380. The stamp commemorated the new Forth Road Bridge, but part of the background was missing.

**Postmarks.** The world's *biggest collection* of different postmarks belongs to R. K. Forster of Scarborough, Yorkshire. He began collecting when he was 16, and had a job checking the mail in for a printing firm. That was in 1931. In a couple of years, with the help of pen-friends, he had collected 700 postmarks from all over the world. He now has about 150,000. There are 437,168 Post Offices in the world, so he has still some way to go before completing his collection.

Postmarks were used on letters many hundreds of years before adhesive stamps, and can be very valuable. A hand-written Post Office note on a letter dated 1661 was sold for £9,000 in a London auction in 1976.

*Modern postmarks* can be collected in many different groups – every post office in one county, for example; or a theme, such as *Food*: Ham, Sandwich, Cucumber, Banana, Oyster, Tomato, Pepper and Salt, etc.; or *Noisy Places* like Barking, Yelling, Clatter, Bangs, Mutters, Knock, Hammer and Tongs; or just downright *Odd and Peculiar Places* like Great Snoring, Freezy Water, Ugley, Up Down Hill, Peculiar, Pincushion and Pennycomequick, Honeymoon and Heart's Content, Ben Hur and Green Gables.

**The last postal place-name in the world** is Zyznow in Poland.

**The highest Post Office in the world** is at Cerro de Pasco in Peru, at 4,384 m above sea-level.

**The most out-of-the-way postmark in Britain** is probably 'Crow Tor Dartmoor', a postmark with a crow on it. The pillar-box is at Cranmere Pool, Dartmoor, and there is no official collection at all.

# Particular and Peculiar Places

## COUNTRIES

**Biggest.** The U.S.S.R. is 22,402,200 sq. km (about 8,650,000 sq. miles) in area. The next biggest country, Canada, would easily fit into it *twice*.

**Most people.** China has about 900 million. If they stood on each other's shoulders, they'd make *three human chains to the moon*.

**Films.** India makes more films than any other country – 619 in 1978. Next biggest film-makers are Japan and then France.

**Television.** Japan *makes* the most televisions – about 14 million a year. The U.S.A. *has* the most – about 123 million. The little country of Monaco has the most televisions in proportion to its people – 607 out of every 1,000 have a telly.

**Mountains.** Nineteen of the twenty highest mountains in the world are in the Himalayas. The range stretches across six countries – Bhutan, China, Nepal, India, Pakistan and Afghanistan.

The Hawaiian Islands are the *tops* of the biggest mountain range in the world. Mauna Kea, on Hawaii, is 33,476 ft high, measuring from base to top, and including the part of it which is under water. (4,000 ft taller than Mount Everest.)

**Driest.** Egypt has 55·8 mm a year of rain. If you stood out all year, the water would just about cover your ankles – unless it all evaporated in the heat and you got sunstroke first.

**Wettest.** Colombia has 4,099 mm of rain a year.

The most *thundery* place in the world is Java in Indonesia, with 322 thundery days a year.

**Hottest.** Mali has an average temperature of 28·3° C – that's all the year round.

**Roads.** The U.S.A. has the most roads – 6 million km. Enough to stretch almost 153 times round the world!

**Railway track.** The U.S.S.R. has 260,000 km.

**Languages.** India has by far the most different languages – about 845.

**Chocolate.** The U.S.A. makes the most – 863,000 tonnes (about 850,000 imperial tons) a year. Switzerland makes and sells enough chocolate for every Swiss to eat two big bars a day.

**Chewing-gum.** The U.S.A. chew the most – 35 billion sticks of chewing-gum a year – twenty-five packets for every man, woman and child.

**Smallest.** The Vatican City in Italy is the smallest. Area: 44 hectares (108.7 acres). Population: about 1,000.

(Unofficially, the smallest country is *Sealand* – a 10 × 25 ft cement fort, built 7 miles off the east coast of Britain in World War II. Roy Bates moved there in 1966 with his wife and son. Mr Bates declared himself King, said Sealand was an independent country and issued stamps, passports and a Sealand dollar.)

# ISLANDS

**Redonda.** Redonda is a small, mountainous, uninhabited island in the Caribbean with one most curious thing – *an English King!* King Juan II of Redonda is Jon Wynne-Tyson, a writer from Sussex, England. King Juan's island is 1 mile long and ½ a mile wide and lies 15 miles N.N.W. of Monserrat.

Columbus discovered it and named it Redonda in 1493. It was briefly inhabited when its phosphates were mined many years ago, but otherwise it was and is a desert island. An Irishman, Matthew Dowdy Shiell, annexed Redonda for his son Matthew, who was crowned King Philip of Redonda on his 15th birthday in 1880. When John Gawsworth, a British author, became King Juan I in 1947, he created a Court of nobles for his desert island. He gave titles to writers and poets like Dylan Thomas, Dorothy Sayers and Ellery Queen, so that Redonda has a Grand Duke, an Archbishop, dozens of Dukes and Duchesses, a Baron, Knights, a Grand Chamberlain, a Master of the King's Horse and a Cartographer Royal. But the *only living things* on King Juan's island are *goats, large rats, lizards, burrowing owls, boobies, huge land crabs and a very prickly cactus.*

King Juan II succeeded in 1970, and in 1979 he made his first kingly visit to his island. On 13 April, accompanied by some of his nobles, including a geologist (now the Duke of Strata), the Grand Duke, the Duke of Waladli and an archaeologist (now the Duke of Artefact), he landed by rubber dinghy on the rocks below the steep and treacherous gully that leads to the summit of the island. They planted a flag on the top at 10.15 and read a short proclamation. This was pinned to the wall of a small timber post office – the only building on the island, put up in 1977. They explored the active volcano, and the Great Alps Waterfall and the old mine-shafts, and breathed in the sulphurous air in the tropical afternoon sun. After two days anchored offshore, King Juan II and his Dukes left the island again to its goats and boobies, taking with them the only piece of civilization left lying there – a 19th-century bottle, now in the Duke of Artefact's collection.

**Cat island.** 1,200 miles south of Cape Town, South Africa, lies the world's most extraordinary island. Only a handful of people live there – meteorologists who work on a weather station. In 1947 they brought five cats to the island, to keep down the rats. By 1976, those five *cats* had had *kittens*, and those *kittens* had had *kittens*, and those first five cats had had so many *great-great-great-grandkittens* that Marion Island is now the world's most cat-populated island, with at least 6,000 cats on one small island – and not one single rat or mouse.

## STRANGE PLACES

**The Great Wall of China.** Built in the 3rd century BC, with a total length of 3,930 miles, at times 39 ft high and 32 ft thick, this is the only man-made structure visible from space. In the Middle Ages guards on the wall were born, grew up, married, died and were buried within it.

**The Saharan Sand Sea.** In central Algeria, there lies the world's most extraordinary sea of sand, with great waves, each almost 3 miles long, rising to peaks 1,410 ft high.

**Panama.** Because of a bend in the isthmus, Panama is the only place in the world where you can see the sun rise in the Pacific Ocean and set in the Atlantic.

**Mount Athos.** The monastery at Mount Athos is the malest place in the world. No female is allowed in it – cocks but not hens, horses but not mares, bulls but not cows. It has been like this for more than 700 years.

# FROGGY SHOWERS, FISHY RAIN
# AND BLOODY SNOW

There have been many reports over the centuries of freak showers of animals and fishes. Sometimes these occur in thunderstorms, or they are caused by distant whirlwinds, which suck up the creatures and whirl them through the sky, and down they come in rain.

**Frogs.** The first frog-fall was reported in Greece in the 4th century. The fall of frogs was so great, it blocked the roads and people were unable to open their front doors.

A shower of hundreds of little frogs fell in Birmingham, England, on 12 June 1954. They bounced off people's umbrellas, scaring everyone with their leaping and bounding.

The most recent recorded frog rain was in July 1979, when it rained frogs on the village of Darganata in Soviet Central Asia.

**Toads.** Showers of little toads are even more widely recorded than frogs.

On a bright clear day in August 1804, a great black cloud suddenly appeared near Toulouse, France and let drop thousands of little toads. (Not at all easy to count hopping toads.) An eye-witness described them as 'tremendously numerous'.

On 5 September 1922, little toads fell on Chalon-sur-Saône for *two days*.

On 23 September 1973, 'tens of thousands' of small toads fell from the sky in a freak storm near the southern French village of Brignoles.

**Fish.** There have been many cases of fish-falls in history. Fifty-three falls have been recorded in Australia alone. The largest fall of fish is probably that in Singapore in February 1861. After an intense rainstorm lasting several days 50 acres of land were found covered with catfish.

**Blood.** Red rain has been reported over the years, but has never been proved to be of blood. It could be caused by the same small sea insect that makes the Red Sea red.

*Red snow* is rare. In 1808, 5 ft of red snow fell in Carniola, Germany.

## HOUSES

**Smallest.** The smallest house in the world was a TUB – Diogenes the Greek lived in one.

**Bottle house.** The biggest bottle house was built by David Brown, at Boswell, B.C., Canada. He collected 500,000 empty embalming fluid bottles from his friends in the funeral business. The bottles are square-shaped. He left the tops on, and laid the bottles in mortar, necks facing inwards. The house is enormous, shaped in a clover-leaf pattern, with circular rooms, three towers, bridges and walls in the garden, all built of bottles. The bottle-ends make a glistening mosaic pattern.

**Tin-can house.** Several tin-can houses have been recorded. One was made at Cornell University, U.S.A., in 12 hrs, with windows made from bicycle wheels covered with polythene. The framework was tins, welded end to end.

**Paper house.** The largest and most famous was built by Elis Stenmann at Pigeon Cove, Massachusetts, U.S.A., between 1922 and 1942. It's a log-cabin type, made out of rolled-up newspapers. Each paper can be removed, unrolled, read and replaced. The walls and roof are covered outside with newspapers pasted and folded. Mr Stenmann also built paper tables, curtains, a piano, a fireplace and a grandfather clock, using about 100,000 copies altogether.

**Underground house.** Baldasare Forestiere, of Fresno, California, U.S.A., dug a house underground for forty years, with pick, shovel and wheelbarrow. There are *ninety* rooms, passages and courts – some 10 ft below, some 22 ft, and some 35 ft. Fruit-trees grow down there in courtyards open to the light. While the temperature outside rises to well over 100°F in the summer, the underground house is 70°F all the year round.

**Rubbishy house.** The biggest house built of junk was made by Art Beal, at Nitwitt Ridge, West Cambria Pines, California, U.S.A. He has been building for forty-five years and still is. The house stretches for 250 ft up a rock face, on nine levels, with two or three rooms on each. It's made of *shells, beer cans, tyres, car wheels, old scrap iron* – every kind of junk. The only materials Mr Beal bought were cement and sand. His neighbours object to the rubbishy look of it, but Mr Beal likes it.

**Bat house.** An anonymous buyer paid £24,000 in 1978 to buy a derelict mansion near Stroud, Gloucestershire – not for himself, but for the greater horseshoe bats in it, so that they could go on living there undisturbed.

**Shoe shop.** A shoe shop in Bakersfield, California, *is* a shoe shop – a white shoe-shape on an elevated sole. *The door is in the toe.*

**Dinosaur shop.** A curio shop in Los Angeles, California, is built in the shape of a dinosaur, almost as large as the Supersaur. *The entrance is in the tail.*

**The Leaning Tower of Chicago.** Outside Chicago, U.S.A., there is a half-size copy of the Leaning Tower of Pisa. Robert Ilg built it in 1931 and lived in it for some time. It is still there.

**Blind man's house.** Francis A. Burdett, an American jeweller, became blind at 50. When he was 63 he began building himself a house, three stories high, with seven rooms and bath, without any assistance whatsoever. He finished it in two and a half years.

**The most horrible house.** Murder Castle was built for Herman Webster Mudgett at 63rd and Wallace Streets, Chicago, in 1893. It had air-tight chambers, secret entrances, false ceilings, rooms lined with asbestos to stifle screams and a death-shaft through which bodies dropped from secret rooms into vats filled with quicklime in the cellar. Mr Mudgett was a murderer in case you didn't guess. He admitted killing 27 people, but detectives say the number was more like 200.

**Most Haunted House.** Borley Rectory, in Essex, was the world's most haunted house. All kinds of spirits and apparitions and weird noises were seen or heard there, including the ghosts of two murdered people, a phantom cat, many footsteps, ringing bells, a hovering brick, many unidentified voices, a nun and a coach and horses driving past the front door. In February 1939 the rectory was burnt to the ground.

## THE WORLD'S WORST SPELLING MISTAKE

America, as everyone knows, is named after Amerigo Vespucci, the Italian navigator. America, after Amerigo.

This seems to be a mistake. An American scholar, George Bijur, working on a book about the Vespucci family, has recently found a signature of Amerigo Vespucci's. He clearly signed himself Emericus Vespucius, the Latin form of his name.

*Emericus vespucius*

So it is also clear that America should be *E*merica, and the U.S.A. must be changed (though it is a bit late now) to the U.S.E.!

# Space and Spirits

## INTO SPACE

**First orbit.** The Russian satellite, *Sputnik*, first orbited the earth, 4 October 1957.

**First man.** Yuri Gagarin, U.S.S.R., made a single orbit in the space vehicle *Vostok*, for 89 mins. on 12 April 1961. Alan Shepard, U.S.A., flew on 5 May 1961.

**First woman.** The first and only woman in space was Valentina Tereshkova, U.S.S.R. She travelled 1,225,000 miles in *Vostok VI*, 16–19 June 1963.

**Space-walker.** Edward H. White, U.S.A., made the first genuine space-walk on 3 June 1965. He opened the hatch of his spacecraft and walked in nothing for 21 mins.

**Man on the moon.** Neil Armstrong, U.S.A., was the first man to step on the moon – 'That's one small step for a man, one giant step for mankind', on 20 July 1969. He stepped out of the Lunar Module *Eagle* on to the Sea of Tranquillity. His footprint may stay there untouched for ever.

**Moon visit.** The longest visit on the moon was made by Capt. Eugene A. Cernan and Dr Harrison H.

Schmitt, U.S.A., in December 1972. They spent 74 hrs 59½ mins. there, collecting moon-rock.

**Fastest humans.** The fastest speed any human being has ever gone was achieved by three American astronauts, Col. Stafford, Cdr Cernan and Cdr Young in the *Apollo X* spacecraft, at a speed of 24,791 m.p.h. (39,897 km/h).

## SPACE ANIMALS

**First.** The first living creature to go into space was a dog called Laika, a Samoyed husky. Laika was the sole passenger in the Russian *Sputnik II*, launched on 3 November 1957. She ran out of oxygen on the flight and died peacefully in space, at a maximum height of 1,050 miles (1,690 km) above the earth. *Sputnik II* reentered the earth's atmosphere after 2,370 orbits, 103 days.

**Space-dogs.** A total of ten space-dogs went into space in the Russian Sputnik programme. In *Sputnik V*, two dogs, Belka and Strelka were orbited together on 19 August 1960 and were successfully recovered by parachute. The last Russian space-dog was Chermushka, launched on 9 March 1961.

**Mice and spiders.** Four black mice were launched into space on 3 December 1959, but the satellite failed to go into orbit. The first true space-mice were launched successfully into orbit in the American *Skylab 3*, on

28 July 1973. *Skylab 3* carried six pocket mice, some minnows and two spiders called Anita and Arabella. Anita and Arabella both managed to spin their webs, despite being in a state of weightlessness.

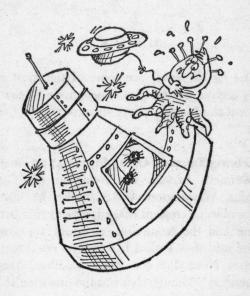

**Tortoises.** Several dozen rats, six boxes of tortoises and four beetles were sent into space as part of the Cosmos project and were recovered after three weeks.

**Monkey.** A pig-tailed monkey called Boney went into space in 1969.

**Frogs.** Two male bullfrogs orbited the earth in 1970. The spacecraft was called *OFO-1* (*Orbiting Frog Otolith*).

**Chimpanzee.** Ham the chimp was launched into space from Cape Canaveral, on 31 January 1961. The flight ran into several problems, but Ham managed to perform all his duties correctly and cheerfully accepted the kind offer of an apple on landing.

## U.F.O.s

Here, *just for the record*, are some of the most extraordinary sightings, and close encounters of the first, second and third kind. Believe them or not, just as you like.

**First 'Flying Saucer'.** On 24 June 1947 an American pilot, Kenneth Arnold, was flying in the Cascade Mountains, Washington, U.S.A., when he saw nine gleaming objects, crescent shaped, zig-zagging between his plane and the mountains, at about 1,400 m.p.h. Later, he said they looked like saucers skimming over the water. Next day the Press headlined them as 'flying saucers'. Though that was the first time U.F.O.s had been *called* flying saucers, queer things in the sky had been noted for hundreds of years. (Some people think Elijah the prophet was taken up into Heaven in a flying saucer.)

**Little green men.** Carlos Diaz, a waiter, was walking home early in the morning of 4 January 1975, near Bahia Blanca in Argentina, when he was paralysed by a beam of light from above. The air hummed and vibrated; he was drawn up and became unconscious.

Four hours later he was found lying by the side of a road 500 miles away and taken to hospital. He said he had woken in a translucent globe with three green men-like creatures, who had painlessly taken tufts of hair out of his head! (And that was true – he *had* lost some hair, the hospital discovered.)

In France in 1965, a lavender farmer, out working at 7 a.m., saw a rugby-football-shaped vehicle, on legs, land in one of his fields. When he got close he saw two small creatures, 3–4 ft high, with big melon-shaped heads, eyes running round the side of the head, no hair, a slit for a mouth, no nose, pointed chins and big, puffy cheeks. One of them pulled out a small stick, pointed it at him, paralysing him for a while, at which point they went up into their vehicle on a shaft of light and took off. To this day, nothing will grow on that patch of ground.

# GHOSTS

**The oldest.** The oldest ghost recorded in Britain came galloping out of the Bronze Age one night on to the Dorset Downs. A Fellow of the Royal Society of Archaeologists was driving on open downland near Sixpenny Handley in Dorset when he saw the horseman riding beside him, with bare legs, a long loose cloak, no bridle or stirrups, and brandishing a stone axe. For about a hundred yards the ancient man pounded along beside the car and then he swerved away and vanished into an ancient burial mound.

**The phantom omnibus.** The phantom bus was a London No. 7 bus, which used to go racing by, all lit-up, without a driver or conductor, through Cambridge Gardens to the junction with St Marks Road, where it dissolved in thin air. A motorist was killed there in 1944, swerving to avoid it, but it has not been seen lately.

**The boy on the train.** This ghost was only seen once. The witness was sitting in a 3rd class compartment of the train between Rye and Winchelsea in Sussex. Opposite him were two other passengers in each corner, and a gap in the middle. Suddenly a small boy appeared in the gap, dressed in old-fashioned clothes, with a big white Eton collar. For quite a while the boy sat there, making awful faces at the man opposite him. Then gradually he began to fade away – first, the man watching saw the pattern of the seat behind begin to appear through his body, and then the boy vanished altogether.

The most curious thing, though, was – the boy had been sitting 6 ins. *above* the seat! The man who saw this apparition thought he must have been sitting on someone's lap.

**The cyclist.** Thomas Eales used to hurtle down the steep hill at Stoneleigh Bridge near Coventry, Warwickshire, right down to a sharp right-angled bend at the bottom. But one day he crashed headlong into the wall and broke his neck. Since then he has been seen again and again, hurtling down and crashing into the wall.

**Fly-boy Willie.** Fly-boy Willie is the nickname of the ghost of a war-time pilot who flew his Wellington bomber on a mission from the R.A.F. station at Lindholme in South Yorkshire. His plane was shot up over Germany and crashed near the Humber on the way back in 1944. Fly-boy Willie was killed, but he got back to base all the same. His Commanding Officer used to see him clumping up the stairs in his flying-boots. And the C.O.'s son saw him, and spoke to him once.

# Mostest

## BIGGEST

**Mammal.** The largest mammal in the world is the blue whale. The largest ever measured was 33·58 m (110 ft 2 ins.) long. *The heaviest* was reckoned to weigh 174 tons. An average blue whale weighs 480 lions, 600 giraffes, 120,000 hedgehogs and 4,800,000 mice.

**Killer whale.** The largest killer whale in captivity is called Orky. He weighs 14,000 lb.; he lives in a salt-water tank at Hanna–Barbera's Marineland, on the Palos Verdes Peninsula, U.S.A., and they *don't* give him people to eat. But he eats *the weight of two people* every day in herrings and mackerel.

**Fish.** The largest fish ever caught on a fishing line was a man-eating great white shark, weighing 2,664 lb. (1,208·4 kg) and 16 ft 10 ins. (5·13 m) long.

**Daddy-long-legs and giant ant.** See end of book. If you are a nervous type, *don't* see end of book.

**Spider.** The biggest spider ever found was a bird-eating spider, found in French Guyana in South America. Its body was 8·9 cm (3·5 ins.) long, and its legs stretched out for 25 cm (9·8 ins.).

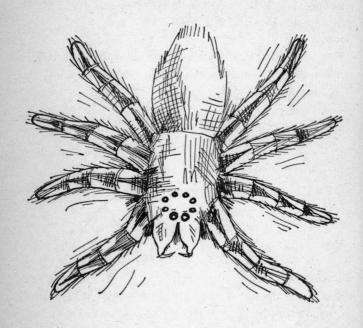

**Living thing.** The biggest living thing in the world is a Sequoia tree called General Sherman, 83 m tall, in the Sequoia National Park, California, U.S.A. Thirteen big men with outstretched arms could just touch fingers round its trunk. If a vandal dared to chop it down, he could make forty five-roomed bungalows or 5,000 million matches with the wood. The seed it grew from is no bigger than $\frac{1}{16}$ in. (1·6 mm).

**Mushroom.** The largest mushroom was found in a field near Lille, France. It was 4 ft high and weighed 12 lb.

**Easter egg.** The biggest Easter egg ever made – *not* chocolate – contained two live ponies pulling a carriage. It wasn't sent through the post – it was wheeled on to the lawn.

**Nutcracker.** The world's largest nutcracker, 8 ft long, hangs outside *the world's only nut museum* in Old Lyme, Connecticut, U.S.A.

**Christmas cracker.** The world's biggest cracker was made for the B.B.C. TV *Record-Breakers* programme in December 1974. It was 45 ft long and 8 ft across.

**Bubble.** The biggest bubble-gum bubble ever blown was $19\frac{1}{4}$ ins. in diameter, blown by Susan Montgomery of California, U.S.A. Nigel Fell, aged 13, blew the biggest breath-taking British bubble – $16\frac{1}{2}$ ins.

**Book.** The longest book in the world is more than a mile long and weighs 728 tons. Each page is a 1-ton slab of stone with the text of the Burmese Bible carved on it. Called the *Kutho Daw* (the Marble Scriptures), the book stands beside the road to Mandalay.

**Library fine.** The largest overdue library fine actually paid was £110 for twenty-two overdue books. Mr and Mrs Anthony Abraham of Bristol had to pay costs as well – a grand total of £153·30.

**Money.** The Yap islanders in the Pacific used the biggest money ever known – giant stone cart-wheels. These were kept under water; the owners changed, but the cart-wheels stayed where they were, because Yap pockets weren't big enough. For ordinary shopping, the islanders used seashells or mother-of-pearl.

**3-figure number.** The biggest 3-figure number is $9^{(9^9)}$, which is 9, raised to the power of 387,420,489, and if you worked *that* out, the final answer would contain 369 million numbers.

**National Anthem.** The Greek National Anthem has 158 verses.

**Matchbox.** The biggest matchbox for sale in England was made by Loncraine Boxton, to hold a match-stick lighter, and was 50 cm long. In 1978 it cost £2. (Matchbox collectors, by the way, are called *cumyxaphists*.)

**Penknife.** The penknife with the most blades is the Sheffield Year Knife, first made in 1822. In 1980 it had 1,980 blades, in 1981 it had 1,981 blades, one for each year. It also has miniature table knives and forks, a hacksaw and nail file, a pair of scissors and a corkscrew. The knife is 80 cm high and 55 cm wide and you can see it in the foyer of Stanley Tools at Woodside in Sheffield. The blades are always kept open because, once closed, it would take a *whole week* to open them all again.

**Tin-opener.** The biggest tin-opener in Britain is 5 ft long, and was used by several people to open the biggest tin can, 5 ft tall and 4 ft wide, to let out Tom Saddinton, who had been tinned inside for two hours. He got in on 28 October 1978 at the Arnolfini Galleries in Bristol and the lid was welded on, but he had two air holes to breathe through.

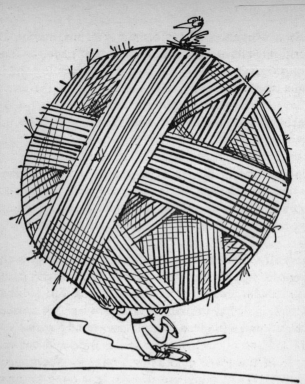

**Ball of string.** The biggest ball of string is 11 ft tall, made by Francis Johnson of Darwin, Minnesota, U.S.A. He was a hay-baler and started rolling in 1950 with saved up bits of baling twine. Now it's rolled up with a hydraulic roller. Mr Johnson says, 'There's solid twine all the way through, though there might be a few acorns inside, since the squirrels like to sit on it.'

**Pencil.** The biggest pencil is a 3B – 7 ft long. It belongs to Tony Hart.

**Suit of armour.** The biggest suit of armour in the world is a suit of *elephant* armour in the Tower of London. It was last used at the Battle of Plassey in 1757 in India and is the only elephant armour in the world today. The armour weighs 262 lb., and is made in six pieces, with beautifully decorated iron plates joined by chain mail. The armour covers nearly all the elephant's body, including his face, with flaps over his big ears and two openings for his eyes. The *Mahout*, or driver, sat on his neck; the warrior sat behind with a rack of weapons; and clinking and clanking, the great Indian elephant swayed into battle.

**Aircraft.** The biggest aircraft ever made, with a wingspan of 97·54 m (320 ft), was a Hercules flying-boat. Howard Hughes had it built, at a cost of $40 million; he flew it once, off Long Beach Harbor, California, U.S.A., and since then it has never flown again.

The *Spruce Goose* flew first (and last) on 2 November 1947. Then it was locked away for 23 years in a sealed hangar. Finally, in October 1980, the colossal doors were opened, the giant flying boat emerged, and was put on display in Long Beach, California.

**Football stadium.** The biggest football stadium is the Maracana Municipal Stadium in Rio de Janeiro, Brazil. It holds 205,000 people.

**Road.** The widest road is the Monumental Axis in Brasilia, Brazil. It is 250 m wide and you could fit 160 cars across it, side by side.

# THE BIGGEST
# CHOCOLATE FACTORIES

The biggest chocolate factory is the Hershey factory, in Hershey, Pennsylvania, U.S.A. Hershey's make Goodies and Twizzlers and Nibnax and Whatchmacallits among other things, but most of all they make the Hershey Bar, the most famous milk chocolate bar in America.

Near the proper factory is a huge Model Factory called Chocolate World. Visitors there step into automated cars and get whisked past all the chocolate-making machines – the cleaners and crushers and refiners and conchers – and right through a roasting oven, just like a cocoa bean.

In the grounds, there's a Hershey School, and the Hershey Bears play ice hockey in the Hersheypark Arena, and the Hershey football team play in the Hersheypark football stadium. The Hersheypark itself has Giant Wheels and roller coasters and a sooperdooperLooper (spelt like that), which turns you upside-down at 66 feet per second, and a Kissing Tower, 330 ft high with a chocolate-coloured cabin on top with kiss-shaped windows, to give chocolate kisses in. There's a chocolate shop too.

The biggest chocolate factory in Britain is Cadbury's Bournville Factory near Birmingham. Cadbury's sell over 200 million cream eggs at Easter – more than three for every single man, woman and child in the country.

## SMALLEST

**Watch.** 1·2 cm long, 0·476 cm wide.

**Television.** $3\frac{1}{2}$ ins. × 2 ins. × 7 ins. Screen 2 ins. square (Sinclair Radionics).

**Book.** 2·1 mm square, 0·8 mm thick (fifteen pages, 'Three Blind Mice').

**Christmas Card.**
A grain of rice, engraved.

**Bicycle.** Wheels 5·4 cm in diameter. It was ridden by Charlie Charles at the Circus Hotel in Las Vegas, U.S.A.

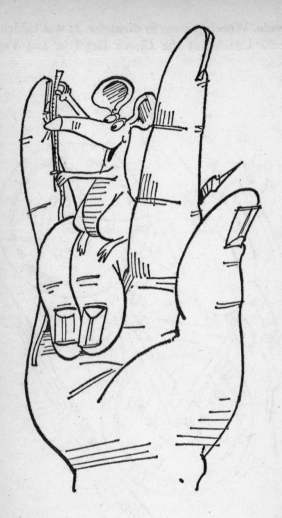

**Unit of measurement.** The attometer. An adult's little finger is about 7,000,000,000,000,000,000 attometers long.

**Model railway.** Goes round a 10p piece on a bottle top.

**The smallest spy.** M. Richeborg was a midget – just about 23 ins. tall – and a servant of the Orléans family in France. At the time of the French Revolution he became a secret agent. The family wrapped him up in baby clothes and put him in his nurse's arms; she carried *him* and *he* carried the secret dispatches, in and out of Paris, tucked into his nappies and nighties, all wrapped round with a shawl.

**Microdots – the world's smallest film.** A microdot film is the size of a full-stop. And that full-stop can contain a message as big as a double-page of this book. Microdots are used by spies to transmit their messages.

Here are three microdots, found in an envelope belonging to the Russian spy, Mrs Helen Kruger who was sentenced to twenty years' imprisonment for spying in Britain.

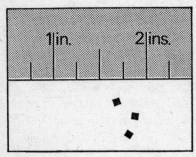

A part of one of them – enlarged – looks like this.

```
    ...КОМУ. ПРИ ОБХО..
    ..АК-ТО ХОРОШО И ПРИЯТН..
    МЕНЯ СПРАШИВАЮТ, А БУДУ Л.
    РАБОТЕ, НА КОТОРОМ Я ПЕЖА "Ж.
    . И КАК-ТО СТАЛО ГРУСТНО-ГРУСТ.
    .ХОДИТСЯ КУДА-ТО СПЕШИТЬ И ЭСЕ
    .СЛЕДНИЙ ДЕНЬ, ПРОВЕДЕННЫЙ В ПРАГ
    .ТО ТЯЖЕЛО И ГРУСТНО СТАЛО И.. И.
    .ОЙ ЧЕТВЕРТИ ОЧЕНЬ ОГОРЧИЛА.ПЕР.
    .ТРОЙКИ:. ПО ГЕОМЕТРИИ, АЛГЕБР.
    .ТЫ НЕ ПРЕДСТАВЛЯЕШЬ, КАК Я
    .С ЕЩЕ ХУЖЕ ОТМЕТКИ, ВКЛ.
    .ОРЯ, ВЕЧЕР ПРОШЕЛ .
```

# FASTEST

**Land animal.** The pronghorn antelope of the Western United States is the fastest. Average speed: 53 m.p.h. over 1 mile. Top speed: 61 m.p.h. for 200 yds.

Next fastest is the cheetah. Top speed: 56 m.p.h.

**Bird.** Fastest flyer is the spine-tailed swift. Top speed: about 106 m.p.h.

Fastest runner is the emu. Top speed: 40 m.p.h.

**Fish.** The American sailfish can reach speeds of 68 m.p.h.

**Human-powered vehicle.** Ralph Therrio won the International Championships in 1977 in California, U.S.A., at a record 49·38 m.p.h.

The two-man event was won in 1978 in the record time of 54·43 m.p.h. The machine was a tricycle called *White Lightning*, covered over and 20 ft long, weighing 75 lb. The two riders lay flat out inside it.

The record for a normal tandem bicycle is 45·5 m.p.h.

**Car.** Stanley Barrett was the first man to break the sound barrier on land, in a rocket car with a Sidewinder missile, at 739·666 m.p.h. on 17 December 1979. (Speed of sound is 731 m.p.h.) He felt a jolt like hitting a brick wall, and a sound like distant thunder lasted for 2 secs. The vehicle had a 48,000 h.p. engine and cost £363,000.

**Aeroplane.** 2,193·167 m.p.h. for a Lockheed SR-71A on 28 July 1976.

A top speed of 4,534 m.p.h., the fastest ever for a fixed-wing plane, was reached by an American X-15A-2 on 3 October 1967.

The Space Shuttle *Orbiter*, which was first flown in 1977, will go at 17,600 m.p.h. when it operates in space.

**Sneeze.** 100 m.p.h.

**Tortoise.** A giant tortoise can go 0·17 m.p.h. (1 mile in nearly 6 hours) at its very fastest, racing to get its dinner.

**Tree-climbing.** 36 secs. up a 90 ft pine.

**Golf ball.** A golf ball, when first hit, was measured to be travelling at a speed of 340 m.p.h.

## COLLECTIONS

**Gnomes.** The biggest collection of garden gnomes in Britain is owned by Ann Atkin, founder of the Gnome Club, at the Gnome Reserve, West Putford, Devon. The most gnomes seen sitting and standing there at one time were 1,500. (That's the most gnomes known – if you know a bigger gnome collection, please let me gnow.)

**Whistles.** Alan Kipping of London, N.W.1, owns 1,200 different whistles.

**Newspapers.** John Frost, 8 Monks Avenue, New Barnet, Hertfordshire, owns the world's biggest private collection of newspapers – a total of 25,000 copies of 7,500 different newspapers. He first began collecting when he was 10, with the news of the R101 airship disaster. His news dates back to 1640, and includes the coronation and death of every British monarch since 1761. He specializes in outstanding world events, with headlines like: NELSON DIES; TITANIC SINKS; MAN ON THE MOON, and his collection includes the world's smallest newspaper – a four-page issue of *The Times*, specially printed for the Queen's Doll's House in 1924; size, $1\frac{1}{2} \times 2\frac{1}{2}$ ins. His most unusual news appears in the *Daily Express*, 23 June 1931, with a great big headline saying:

THE WORLD ENJOYS A CHEERFUL DAY.

**Rock stars' socks.** Tony Valence, of the Isle of Sheppey, Kent, has a unique collection of forty pairs of American rock stars' socks. He started collecting by offering Little Richard £10 for his socks. Little Richard took them off and handed them over right away, including the holes in the toes. Mr Valence keeps his collection in a sealed polythene bag, but hangs them out on the washing line for an airing every now and then. His collection includes a black pair with white guitars belonging to Jerry Lee Lewis.

**Rubbers.** Irena Berglas aged 12, of Barnet, has a collection of about 400 pencil-rubbers, all different, including a bubble-gum-smelling rubber, and a working yo-yo rubber.

**Pencil-sharpeners.** The largest collection of pencil-sharpeners in Britain numbers over 500, all different, belonging to Alan and Susie Fuller of Streatham, London.

**Chamber-pots.** The biggest collection of chamber-pots in Britain, totalling 650, belongs to Joe Painter of Lancashire. (Chamber-pots are grown-up potties, made of china. Hotel bedrooms used to have them in bedside cupboards or hiding under the bed. In the morning the chamber-maids would carry the chamber-pots *very carefully* along the passages to the bathroom.)

**Moustache-cups.** One of the most unusual collections is a collection of 120 moustache-cups, belonging to Gregory Cutshaw of Chorley, Lancashire. Moustache-cups were specially designed so that gentlemen didn't wet their whiskers while drinking their cuppas.

**Football programmes.** Football programmes are very keenly collected, with very high prices paid for some copies. The 1923 Cup Final programme, the first at Wembley, originally cost 3d, but is now worth over £100. Marvin Berglas of Barnet has possibly the largest collection in Britain, with over 10,000, including the oldest Cup Final Programme, for the match in 1890, now worth over £300, and every Arsenal programme for every match played both at home and abroad since 1945.

## RECORD RECORDS

**Milk chocolate disc.** Albert Whelan, an Australian comic, recorded some songs in Germany in 1902 on milk chocolate. The records were too soft to replay – you played the record *and then ate it.*

**Smallest.** The smallest record was made by H.M.V. in 1924. It is 3·5 cm in diameter and plays 'God Save the King'.

**Thickest.** Duophone in 1927–8 issued records so thick that they could be sliced in half and each side played separately.

**Postcard records.** A set of picture postcards, issued by Raphael Tuck in 1929, had a tiny record pressed into it, playing tunes like 'D'ye ken John Peel', for 1 min.

**Cigarette card records.** A packet of twenty Record Cigarettes in 1934 contained a square record, 3 × 3 ins., with a round track.

**Youngest gold disc.** Osamu Minaga wa of Tokyo, Japan, aged 6, for the record single *Kuro Neko No Tango* – 'The Black Cat Tango'.

## MOTORCYCLES

**First.** First two-wheeler – 1869, made by Michaux of France. Steam-powered, with solid tyres, the rider sat in a hot seat above the red-hot boiler!

First petrol-driven bike – 1885, made by Daimler, Germany. Top speed – 12 m.p.h.

First commercial bike – 1894, made by Hildebrand and Wolfmüller. It had a twin-cylinder 4,488 cc engine and still holds the record for the *largest engine ever fitted to a production bike*. The mudguard held water to cool it.

**Silver Bird.** Don Vesco's Silver Bird set the *world speed record* on Bonneville Salt Flats, Utah, U.S.A., 28 September 1975 (still unbroken in 1981).

Highest speed – 307·692 m.p.h. (about 495 km/h).
Flying mile – 303·810 m.p.h. Time – 11·8495 secs.

Silver Bird has two Yamaha TZ750 engines and is 21 ft long. Don Vesco lies flat out inside. The cockpit top is only 81 cm above ground. The bodywork is 1·5 mm-thick aluminium. It has two skids on each side and two brake parachutes.

**Jumping.** Eddie Kidd holds the world record for:
Longest jump (staying in full control of bike) – 190 ft.
Jumping fourteen double-decker buses.

Vicki Muxlow, aged 6, has jumped sixteen people on her hotted-up 50 cc motorbike. Police stopped her attempt to jump seventeen people in August 1979 as too dangerous – for her, not them!

**The Imps.** Junior motorcycle display team. Founded in 1974. It has twenty-eight members from Hackney, London, aged 6–16. They perform formation rides, pyramids, big jumps and fire jumps on a fleet of Honda XL125s and XR75s.

# Endurance
# and
# Survival

## LONG-DISTANCE
## AND ENDURANCE RECORDS

**Stilt-walking.** Sylvain Dornon walked 1,830 miles from Paris to Moscow in fifty days in 1891.

Emma Disley, aged 12, of Hampton, Middlesex, stilt-walked up Snowdon in 4½ hrs, 19 August 1977.

**Walking on water.** Sergeant Walter Robinson, U.S.A., 'walked' across the Channel in 11½ hrs on home-made water shoes, 25 August 1978.

**Roller-skating.** Clinton Shaw roller-skated 4,900 miles from Victoria, B.C., to St John's, Newfoundland on the Trans-Canadian Highway, 1 April to 11 November 1967.

**Go-karting.** A go-kart with a clearance of 2 ins. above the ground went 23,000 miles through twenty-eight countries, starting from New York, 15 February 1961 and ending in New York, 5 June 1964.

**Walking on hands.** Johann Hurlinger of Austria walked on his hands for 871 miles (10 hrs a day for fifty-five days) at an average of 1·58 m.p.h. (2·4 km/h) from Vienna to Paris in 1900.

**Toy balloon.** A toy balloon flew 9,000 miles from Atherton, California, U.S.A., to Pietermaritzburg, S. Africa, 21 May to 10 June 1972.

**Hot-air balloon.** Ben Abruzzo, Max Anderson and Larry Newman, U.S.A., in *Double Eagle II* were the first men to fly the Atlantic in a balloon. They flew 3,000 miles from Albuquerque, New Mexico, in 137 hrs, landing in Evreux, France, on 17 August 1978. Eighteen other balloons had failed and five men had lost their lives in the attempt.

**Human-powered flight.** The *Gossamer Condor*, pedalled by Bryan Allen won the £50,000 Kremer prize for the first official man-powered flight on 23 August 1977 in California. On 12 June 1979 Bryan Allen pedalled *Gossamer Albatross* across the Channel. The flying bicycle had a 96 ft wingspan, weighed 55 lb. and took 2 hrs 49 mins. for the 23-mile flight. Bryan Allen produced 0·23 h.p. to get it there, and Dr Paul Mac-Cready, the designer, won the £100,000 Kremer prize.

**Cross-country running.** Mansen Ernst, a Norwegian, ran from Paris to Moscow in two weeks, swimming thirteen large rivers and averaging 125 miles a day. In a race from Constantinople (Istanbul) to Calcutta and back – 5,625 miles altogether – he averaged 95 miles a day for 59 days.

**Solo rowing.** John Fairfax, G.B., first rowed the Atlantic from East to West in 180 days in 1969. He and Sylvia Cook were the first to row the Pacific together, in 362 days from 26 April 1971 to 22 April 1972.

The first solo Pacific rower was Anders Svedlund of Sweden. He took 118 days in 1974.

*No one has yet rowed round the world.*

**Reverse motoring.** Charles Creighton and James Hargis drove a Ford Model A car from New York City to Los Angeles without stopping the car once. They then drove right back again. In fact, the whole trip – 7,180 miles in forty-two days – was made *backwards*.

**The walking violinist.** Otto E. Funk, aged 62, walked from New York City to San Francisco, California, U.S.A., 4,165 miles, playing his violin all the way.

**Milk-bottle on head.** Willie Hollingsworth, U.S.A., walked 29·7 km (17·2 miles) with a full pint bottle of milk on his head.

**Leap-frogging.** Fourteen members of Hanover High

School, New Hampshire, U.S.A., spent 148 hours in 1978, leap-frogging for 888·9 km (555·25 miles).

**Butterflying.** A monarch butterfly flew 3,009 km (1,869·7 miles) from Eastern Canada to Luis Potosi, Mexico.

**Arrow.** Henry Drake, U.S.A., shot an arrow with a foot-bow, while lying on his back, a record distance of 1 mile, 101 yds, 21 ins. (about 1·7 km).

**North Pole.** At 4.45 a.m. precisely on 1 May 1978, Mr Naomi Uemura, the Japanese explorer, became the first person to reach the North Pole single-handed. He has also climbed the highest peaks of five continents, including Mt Everest.

**Round Britain walk.** John N. Merrill walked 6,284 miles all round the coastline of Britain from 3 January to 8 November 1978. He climbed the three highest mountains on the way, ate 1,511 bars of chocolate, drank 529 pints of milk and wore out 33 pairs of socks and 3 pairs of boots.

**Channel-swimming.** On 7 August 1979 Marcus Hooper of Greenwich, London, became the youngest person to swim the British Channel. He was 12 years old on 14 July. The crossing took 14 hrs 37 mins.

The first 12-year-old to swim the Channel was Kevin Anderson of South Africa – he is three months older than Marcus, but he swam the channel 27 hrs earlier.

**Parachuting.** David Parchment of Oxford fell a total of 66 miles in 233 parachute jumps in 18 hrs 7 mins., in June 1979. He jumped through the night by searchlight.

**Hang-gliding.** In 1979 Jean-Marc Boivin, an Alpine guide from Dijon, France, climbed the second highest mountain in the world – K2 in the Himalayas, and then jumped off the summit (7,600 m above sea-level) with his hang-glider. He came hang-gliding down at speeds of 80 m.p.h. in 13 mins. It took him four months to walk up the mountain.

Boivin was given a £100,000 gold laurel wreath for this, as winner of the international award for Valour in Sport in February 1980. (That wreath went into the bank and he kept a £5,000 replica.) Other finalists included Marcus Hooper and Paul Crump, 15, a young cricketer from Merthyr Tydfil, Glamorgan, who though he has only one arm, scored two centuries and took thirty-five wickets for his cricket club.

**Round-the-world.** David Springbett went round the world in January 1980 from Los Angeles, via London, Bahrain, Singapore, Bangkok, Manila, Tokyo, Honolulu and back to Los Angeles in a record 44 hrs 6 mins., on scheduled air flights. He beat even an American B152 bomber (with a time of 45 hrs 19 mins.) to become *the fastest man in the atmosphere.*

**Brick-smashing.** A karate instructor, Thomas Slaven of Sydney, Australia, has smashed a record 4,487 bricks with one hand in an hour.

**Radio-controlled helicopter.** A radio-controlled model helicopter crossed the Channel for the first time in July 1974, flying from Ashford in Kent to Ambleteuse in France. Flying time was 1 hr 13 mins. The helicopter was a German Bell 212 kit, controlled by Dieter Ziegler, who followed his model, directing it above the waves, all the way across, from the cabin of a full-size helicopter.

**Camping-out.** Graeme Hurry of the 38th Coventry Central Scout Group set a British record on 19 June 1978, when he came indoors to sleep on a real bed for the first time in four years. He had been camping-out for exactly four years and forty-six days.

In 1980, three other Scouts were still camping-out, in an effort to break that record. David Ross of Manchester started camping in 1977, and so did Michael Briggs of Bridgwater. Jason Wright, an 11-year-old Cub of the 1st Horndon-on-the-Hill group in Essex, started in June 1976 – came inside again – and then went out to stay on 5 April 1977. Since then he has worn out two tents and three fly-sheets. At one time it was so cold outside that the zips on his tent froze and his mother had to defrost them to let him out. He has his golden retriever, Crispin, and Badger, his cat, to help keep him warm.

## STRONG MEN AND WOMEN

**Greatest lift by a woman.** 3,564 lb. was lifted by Josephine Blatt in Hoboken, New Jersey, U.S.A., 1895.

**Greatest lift by a man.** 6,270 lb. (a table covered with car parts and a safe full of lead) was back-lifted off the ground by Paul Anderson in Toccoa, Georgia, U.S.A., 1957.

**Horse-pulling.** Louis Cyr withstood the pulling of four horses – two on each arm – in opposite directions. (Montreal, Canada, 1891.) His chest measurement was 59 ins. (150 cm).

**Horse-carrying.** William Pagel carried a 1,000 lb. horse up a set of two 12 ft ladders in 1900.

**Single finger.** Warren L. Travis, U.S.A., lifted 667 lb. with one finger, and 1,105 lb. with two. (Brooklyn, New York, 1907.)

**Pack of cards.** Paul von Boeckmann tore a hole through a pack of cards with a thumb and forefinger in New York, 1900. He also did three chin-ups, pulling his whole weight up, until his chin was touching a top parallel bar, using only the middle finger of his right hand.

**Cannon-ball.** Frank 'Cannonball' Richards withstood a 104 lb. cannon-ball fired into his stomach at close range from a 12 ft cannon. Photographs show the ball hitting his stomach, like a fist hitting a cushion. (Los Angeles, California, 1920.)

## SURVIVORS

**Falls.** Flt Sgt Nicholas Alkemade jumped from a blazing R.A.F. Lancaster bomber on 23 March 1944, at 18,000 ft, *without a parachute*. He fell on to a fir tree, slithered off and landed in a snow bank, without breaking a bone in his body.

A Russian pilot has baled out at 22,000 ft without a parachute, but he was very badly injured.

On 3 December 1979, Elvita Adams jumped from the 86th floor of the Empire State Building, 1,248 ft high. The wind blew her on to a ledge on the 85th floor and a guard pulled her to safety. Only one other person has jumped from the 86th floor and survived.

**Lightning.** Roy C. Sullivan, a Virginia Park Ranger, has been struck by lightning seven times without bad injury: 1942 – lost a big toe nail; July 1969 – eyebrows singed; July 1970 – left shoulder burned; April 1972 – hair set on fire; August 1973 – new hair burned; June 1976 – ankle injured; June 1977 – chest burns.

**Snakes.** Peter Snyman spent fifty days in a small glass and brick cage in a snake park near Johannesburg, S. Africa, with twenty-four of the world's deadliest snakes. He had a break of 20 mins. outside the cage each day – otherwise he spent every minute with his companions – six black mambas, six Egyptian cobras, six puff adders and six boomslangs (tree snakes). He came out on 27 May 1979 and said: 'Thank God, that's over. I couldn't have taken another day.' The snakes said nothing.

**Castaway.** Poon Lim, a Chinese ship steward, spent a record 133 days at sea on a raft. The raft had food for 50 days. He saved rain water and caught fish with a bent nail prised out of the wooden raft.

**Wasps.** 17-month-old Mark Bennet of Vancouver, B.C., survived 447 wasp stings in September 1951. But he had to spend twenty days in hospital.

**Jungle-living.** A Japanese soldier, Yokoi Shoichi, was discovered in 1972 hiding in the jungles of Guam, living on rats, snails, frogs, insects and wild nuts. He had been there since the end of World War II in 1945, but had been afraid to come out. After his rescue, he married and *spent his honeymoon in Guam!*

**James in the whale.** In February 1891 the whaling ship, *Star of the East*, was sailing near the Falkland Isles, when it launched a boat to go harpooning a whale. The boat overturned; one man drowned; another, James Bartley, disappeared.

A few hours later a whale was killed, and the crew spent all day and part of the night cutting it up. Next morning they got to the stomach, and found James Bartley, unconscious, bleached white, doubled up inside. Later, he remembered nothing except incredible heat. It took him three weeks to recover. (This was reported at the time – experts say it's impossible.)

**Atlantic crossing.** Dr Alain Bombard of France is the only man to cross the Atlantic alone, without taking any food or water with him. He set sail on 19 October

1952 in a 5 m dinghy, from Las Palmas in the Canary Islands, taking with him a knife, some string, oars, a fruit-juice squeezer and a small-meshed net.

For the first few days he caught no fish, so he drank a little sea-water. It didn't rain for three weeks. After that he ate raw fish, squeezed the water out of them in his squeezer and drank that. He also ate a spoonful of plankton every day, caught in his net. Finally, on 23 December, weak and very thin, Bombard staggered ashore at Barbados, proving that a ship-wrecked sailor could survive an Atlantic crossing.

**The basic army survival kit** can be contained in a *matchbox*: one fish-hook, one razor blade, a big polythene bag, chalk, a needle, a balloon and waxed matches.

**Luckiest escape.** On 6 January 1918 Capt. J. H. Hedley of Chicago was flying as observer in a fighter plane piloted by a Canadian, Lieut. Makepeace. The plane was attacked by a German fighter and made a sudden vertical dive. Capt. Hedley fell out; dropped down through the sky; landed on the tail of the very plane he had just fallen out of; climbed back into the plane and eventually landed safely.

The official log-book stated: 'Jan. 6. 1918 Mach No. 7255. Height 15,000 ft. Lieut. Makepeace reports Captain J. H. Hedley accidentally thrown into air, afterwards alighted on tail same machine and rescued.'

**The man who *nearly* survived.** Carol Hargis of San Diego, California, put LSD into her husband's toast;

served him blackberry pie containing the venom sac of a tarantula spider; placed bullets in the carburettor of his lorry; tossed a live electric wire into his shower; injected air into his veins with a hypodermic needle to induce a heart attack. But Mr Hargis was *all right*. So she dropped tranquillizers in his beer and smashed him with a steel weight. He didn't survive that. Mrs Hargis was given a life sentence.

## DESERT ISLAND RECORDS

**Living alone on a desert island.** The record is four years four months. Alexander Selkirk, a sailor, had a row with his captain and asked to be put ashore on empty Juan Fernandez Island, west of Valparaiso, South America. Then he changed his mind – 'Take me with you!' – but the ship sailed without him. That was September 1704. He was taken off on 12 February 1709 and eventually got back to Britain. Daniel Defoe, the writer, heard about him and in 1719 wrote his own story based on Selkirk's called *The Adventures of Robinson Crusoe*.

**Desert island horse.** In 1904 a ship carrying a race-horse, Moifaa, from New Zealand to England was sunk in a storm, and Moifaa was washed ashore on a desert island. He wandered alone there until he was rescued two weeks later; got back to England; entered the Grand National – and won by eight lengths.

(If any other horse has been castaway alone on a desert island, he hasn't told anyone about it.)

# Stunts
# and
# Other Lunacies

## DAREDEVILS AND BARNSTORMERS

In the early days of flying and movie-making, airmen and women and stunt men and women did the most hair-raising, record-making stunts that have never been repeated. They flew planes, and crashed them and walked on them, without wires or parachutes. Everything was live – and lots of them died.

**Ormer Lester Locklear** walked the wings of planes by searchlight, *at night, without a parachute*. He also made the first public transfer from plane to plane in mid-air. He changed planes at 2,500 ft and then dropped to the roof of a speeding train.

**Daredevil Al Wilson** replaced the wheel of a crippled plane, while standing on the wing of another, flying beneath it.

**Gladys Ingle** gave archery demonstrations. She stood on one wing tip of a plane; *the target* was at the end of the other wing. It was windy up there, and not exactly steady.

**Earl Daugherty** made the first aerial refuelling. He hopped from one plane to another, in 1921, with a can of petrol. (He was married in the air, too.)

**Snub Pollard,** a Keystone Cop, reckoned he had –
    Bathed in 10 tons of very wet cement
    Caught 14,000 pies full in the face
    Been kicked by a giraffe
    Been hit by over 600 cars and 2 trains.

**Clyde Beatty and the Wrestling Tiger.** In the film 'Darkest Africa' (1936) Clyde Beatty had to wrestle a tiger with his bare hands down a pit. Bobby the Wrestling Tiger was supposed to be well-trained, but he forgot. He charged Beatty over and over again, pinning him down. There was Beatty – under 500 lb. of tiger, yelling and screaming, belting him on the chin, fighting for his life. Finally the attendants managed to open a gate and let the tiger out. The producer, B. Reeves Eason, leaned over the top of the pit and shouted: 'Boy – that was swell. Get your breath, Clyde, and we'll do a re-take . . .' (Beatty didn't do it again – that was a one-and-only, *world's worst stunt.*)

**Stunt Wonder Woman.** Kitty O'Neil is American, pretty, dark-haired, deaf, the stand-in for TV's Wonder Woman, and the world's most intrepid stuntwoman. Altogether she holds thirty-one world records.

In 1976 she became the fastest woman on land when she drove a 48,000 h.p. rocket-powered three-wheeler at 524·019 m.p.h. (843 km/h) in the Alvard Desert in Oregon, U.S.A. In 1980 she made a world-record jump of 180 ft, leaping out of a helicopter without a parachute. She jumped out standing up, then fell down head first, finally flipping over to land on her back, hitting a 30 by 60 ft air-cushion at 60 m.p.h. This is the *highest deliberate stunt leap on to land ever made.*

## NIAGARA WALKERS
## AND OTHER STUNTS

**First.** The first man to walk on a tight-rope over

the Niagara Falls rapids was a Frenchman who called himself Blondin – the most famous tight-rope walker of all time.

The rope was 3 ins. thick, 3,000 ft long, and 230 ft above the rapids. It sagged down in the middle, so there was a 40 ft slope down one end, and a 40ft climb up the other end. It swayed in the wind, too.

Blondin first walked on 30 June 1859. He took 15 mins. to go and 7 mins. to come back.

Blondin went across in many record-making ways:

Blindfold, pushing a woman in a wheelbarrow.

Carrying a man on his back (twice). One man was nervous and wriggled about. 'Sir,' said Blondin, 'I must ask you to sit still, or I will have to put you down.'

He lay down half-way across and did a backward somersault.

He stood on his head.

He took out a small stove to the middle of the rope, cooked himself an omelette and ate it.

He took a chair, balanced it on two legs and sat down.

He went across on stilts – and on a bicycle – and with both hands and legs shackled.

**Woman.** First and only woman to cross was a beautiful Italian acrobat, Maria Spelterina. She did many of Blondin's feats, and two new ones. She walked with her feet in baskets, and she went across backwards.

**Washerwoman.** On 5 September 1860 Enrico Farini, an Italian, dressed up as a washerwoman; took a washing-machine, 6 ft high and weighing almost 100 lb., plus some washing, out to the middle of the rope; drew up water from the river; washed the clothes; hung them on the line, and left them there.

'If anyone thinks they're not clean,' he told the audience, 'they can go out and have a look.'

Thousands and thousands stood on the cliffs watching the Niagara walkers. At that time, it was the Greatest Show on Earth.

**Barrels.** The first person ever to go over the Horseshoe Falls at Niagara in a barrel – a steel drum – *and live* was an American school-teacher, Annie Edison Taylor, on 24 October 1901.

It was another ten years before a *man* dared to try. On 25 July 1911, an Englishman, Bobby Leach, rolled over in an 8-ft steel drum. He broke both knee caps and his jaw and suffered internal injuries. But he lived to be 70. He died in February 1926, in Christchurch, New Zealand, *as a result of slipping on an orange skin*.

Since 1962, police have patrolled the banks of the Falls, to prevent such dangerous stunts, so these Niagara records will probably never be broken.

## LIVE MUMMIES

The *world's worst* living mummy was an anonymous stunt man, working as a double in a mummy film.

He was stripped and wrapped from head to foot in linen bandages, his arms strapped flat beside him, and put in an upright coffin with the door open. He couldn't move; all he could do was stand.

Then they sprayed him with paint and messed up the bandages, to make him look old, and left him to dry. He stood there, sweating, dying for a drink of water and longing to go to the lavatory. Lunchtime came, but they left him there, not wanting to go to all the bother of wrapping him up again.

They started filming after lunch, but one of the actors kept forgetting his lines, and they shot re-take after re-take. By the end of the afternoon the mummy was a raving maniac – and then he fainted. The prop man wildly tore off his bandages and doused him with cold water. He went home and shook for two days and suffered from claustrophobia for the rest of his life.

# Fun and Games

## VERY SPECIAL AND MOST UNUSUAL OLYMPIC RECORDS

**The very first Olympic Games** were held at Olympia, Greece, about 776 BC, and every 4th summer for more than 1,000 years. Even wars never stopped them.

Competitors – amateurs *and* professionals. All competitors competed *naked*.

Prizes – a wreath of olive leaves for the winner. *No* second or third prizes. The winners were heaped with honours – like free dinners in the town hall and a pension for life.

Women – *no* women could compete or watch. One woman caused a sensation in 404 BC. She wanted to watch her son boxing, so she dressed up as a trainer. She got so excited when he won that she leapt over the barrier and everyone saw she was a woman. The judges let her off – but from then on there was a new rule: *all trainers must be naked* in the stadium, too!

**The first modern Games** were held in Athens, Greece, in 1896.

There were only nine sports, including tennis. The men's tennis doubles were won by an Englishman and his German partner. (National teams began in 1912.)

Swimming competitions weren't held in a heated swimming pool, but in the cool waters of the Bay of Zea.

*The oddest medal* was won by George Robinson of England – for reciting a Greek poem in honour of the Games.

**Roque.** The most mysterious Olympic sport. Three Americans won gold, silver and bronze in the Roque event at St Louis in 1900. But nobody knows for sure what it was – something to do with *croquet*, played on a hard surface? Roque has never appeared in any Olympics again.

**King.** King Constantine of Greece is the only king to win an Olympic medal – a yachting gold in 1960.

**False starts.** In 1912, there were eight false starts before the 100 metres finally got going – an Olympic record.

**Tarzan.** Johnny Weissmuller won five Olympic swimming gold medals and broke twenty-seven world records. Then he turned professional, and in 1932 he became the most famous film Tarzan of all.

**First woman.** First woman to win an Olympic gold medal was Charlotte Cooper of England. She won the women's tennis singles in Paris in 1900.

**The 12th Olympic Games.** These games should have taken place in 1940 but were cancelled because of World War II. But some Allied prisoners in the sick-quarters of Stalag XIII, a German prisoner-of-war camp near Nuremberg, decided they should go ahead. So, on 1 September 1940, George O'Brien, a British soldier, declared the Games open, and a Polish duet sang the Olympic anthem.

Events included: *netball* – though the guards put a stop to that; *long jump* over a drainage ditch; *archery*; *cycling* on a frame made from two stools; and *frog-jumping* over 50 m.

A Senegalese won the archery; the shotput (a stone) was won by a Norwegian; a Yugoslav won the long jump; and the Poles won the frog-jumping. French, Dutch and Belgian soldiers also competed.

**Youngest.** Marjorie Gestring, U.S.A., won a gold medal for diving, aged 13 years 9 months.

An unknown French boy won a gold medal, as a cox in a rowing event in 1900, when he was less than 10 years old.

Magdalena Colledge is the youngest ever British competitor. She skated in the 1932 Games when she was only 11 years 24 days old.

# JUST A FEW FOOTBALL RECORDS

**Fastest goal.** 6 secs. Three British footballers share this record: Albert Mundy, Barrie Jones and Keith Smith.

Pat Kruse headed an own goal in the same time – 6 secs.

**Top score.** In an under-14 league match – Midas F.C. v. Courage Colts – in Kent, Courage scored a goal, and then Midas scored 59. Kevin Graham of Midas scored 17. Final score: Midas 59, Courage Colts 1.

The highest score ever recorded in a football match was in the last League game of the season, between Ilinden F.C. and Mladost of Yugoslavia in 1979. Ilinden needed a big score to help their goal average and get promotion. The opposing team, Mladost, and the referee all helped to oblige and Ilinden won by 134–1.

**Youngest League player.** Eamonn Collins played for Blackpool on 9 September 1980 aged 14 years, 323 days. He came on as a substitute in the final 15 minutes of the game against Kilmarnock. (Eamonn is Irish and Irish boys can leave school before they're 16 if they've got a job to go to.)

**Youngest League scorer.** Ronnie Dix, 15 years 180 days.

**Youngest captain.** Terry Neill captained Arsenal when he was 20 and Northern Ireland when he was 21.

**Most goals.** Pelé of Brazil scored 1,216 goals in 1,254 games.

Bobby Charlton scored *forty-nine goals for England.*

**F.A. Cup-winners.** Only side to win seven times – Aston Villa.
Newcastle United has won six times and been in the final eleven times.

Only two sides have won the F.A. Cup *and* League Championship in the same season this century – Tottenham Hotspur in 1961 and Arsenal in 1971.

**League Championships.** Liverpool has won a record

eleven times, with a record sixty-eight points in 1978/9.

**Fastest hat-trick.** Tony Bacon scored a hat-trick in 63 secs. in a high-school game in New York in 1975.

John McIntyre scored four goals in 5 mins. at Blackburn in 1922.

**Most League goals in a season.** Dixie Dean scored a record sixty goals for Everton in League matches in the 1927/8 season. He died in March 1980 – watching Everton play at Goodison Park.

**Smallest player.** The smallest professional footballer in England was Fred LeMay. He was 1·53 m (5 ft) high and weighed only 51 kg (112·4 lb.).

**Goalkeepers.** The *tallest* goalkeeper was Albert Iremonger, who played for Notts County and was 1·96 m (6 ft 5 ins.).

The *heaviest* goalkeeper was Billy Foulke of Sheffield United. He was called Fatty Foulke and Little Willie and he weighed 159 kg (350·5 lb.). He once got a bit annoyed with an opposing centre forward, so he simply lifted him right up off the ground and turned him upside down. Once he got to the tea table after a match before anyone else and ate his team's entire meal.

**The World Cup and Pickles.** The Jules Rimet World Cup Trophy is 12 ins. tall, weighs 9 lb. and is made of solid gold. It was brought to England in 1966, when the Finals were held in this country, and some months before the competition it was put on display during a stamp exhibition in the Central Hall, Westminster. On 21 March it was stolen out of its glass case. The whole footballing world was aghast. *No cup to present for the Final!* No one had any idea where to look for it, except for a little black and white mongrel dog called Pickles.

On 28 March Pickles was taking his owner, David Corbett, for a walk and sniffing round the back gardens of Norwood, North London, when he found it, wrapped up in newspaper and lying on the ground. The cup was returned and Pickles was a hero. He got his pictures in all the papers and a reward – a year's free supply of dog meat and a film contract. What's more, England won the World Cup that Pickles found. They beat West Germany on 30 July. Geoff Hurst of West Ham scored a hat-trick in the match – *the only hat-trick ever scored in a World Cup Final.*

## CURIOUS CRICKET

**Most runs off one ball.** At a junior Eton game, the ball sped to the outfield where the heavy roller was rolling, got rolled on, and by the time they'd got a spade to dig it out – the batsman had scored forty-eight runs.

The famous cricketer C. B. Fry hit a ball which lodged in the fork of a tree. (It was still visible and so *not* a lost ball.) By the time they'd got a ladder, he'd scored sixty-six runs.

(The official record: most runs in one *over* – Gary Sobers hit six sixes for thirty-six in 1968.)

**Oddest match.** In 1796, at Greenwich Hospital, where the old sailors lived, there was a cricket match between those with one arm and those with one leg. The one-legged won by 103 hops.

During the 1979–80 England tour in Australia ... Lillee, bowled Willey, caught Dilley.

**Worst scores.** Many sides have been bowled out for no score, but some have been bowled out more quickly than others. On 11 March 1964 Masterton Central Primary School, New Zealand, dismissed Masterton West School for no runs in *eighteen* balls.

There are two occasions on record when the side out for nought went on to lose the match *without the other side having to hit one single run*. In one match, the captain's first ball was a wide. In the other match, the first bowler bowled a leg-by, first ball, which went to the boundary for four runs.

**Lord's cricket ground** has moved three times – literally. Each time the site was moved, the original turf was dug up and moved too.

# MONOPOLY

**First.** Monopoly was invented by Clarence Darrow in 1933 in America. He chose Atlantic City, New Jersey, for the properties on his board, because that's where he used to spend his holidays and it was his favourite town. He printed 5,000 copies himself. Since then about 100 million have been sold, in fifteen languages. A Chinese version is on sale in Hong Kong. It is *not* for sale in Russia.

**Longest game.** Sixty students in Atlanta, Georgia, U.S.A., played for 1,176 hours. The longest game with four players – 288 hours.

**Largest.** In May 1976 twenty-six teams of scouts played a game using the actual streets and stations in London. They acted as pieces on the board, moving round by tube, bus and on foot. When they passed G O (the Scout Headquarters in Marylebone), they received £200 plus 2p. The 2p was to telephone and report they had truly got there.

The largest indoor game was played on a board 52 ft square in a shopping centre in Flint, Michigan, U.S.A. The players were professional athletes.

**Underwater.** An American high-school group of scuba divers played under water for 72 hrs, on a specially waterproofed board, with weighted pieces. They actually played for 102 hrs but had to surface

briefly after 30 hrs, because of a violent thunderstorm.

**Money.** Over £1,200 million has been printed.

**Most expensive property.** On the English board a house in Mayfair costs £200. Today the smallest mews house (a converted stable) would cost £¼ million and a large house about £3 million.

In the French version, the most expensive property is the Rue de la Paix, in Paris; in the American version it is Boardwalk, in Atlantic City, New Jersey.

**Championships.** First held in Britain in 1975. The first round was held on Platform 3, Fenchurch Street Station. The games started at 11.30 a.m. At 11.38 a.m. one competitor was bankrupt. The final was held in Park Lane.

First World Championships were held in Washington D.C. First winner was John Mair, the Irish Champion, a Dublin merchant banker.

## CHESS

On 11 January 1980, Nigel Short, aged 14, beat grandmaster Ulf Andersson in a 10-hr battle to become Britain's youngest ever *international master*.

A Scottish doctor and his friend in Australia have been playing chess together for over twenty years, making a new move by post every Christmas. The *longest game* still goes on.

Branimir Brebrich of Canada played 575 games *continuously* in 28 hrs against different people, winning 533.

Vlastimil Hort of Czechoslovakia played 201 people *simultaneously* and didn't lose once.

**Living chess.** Living chess games are the world's *biggest* – all the pieces are people.

The *first* game was played in Granada in 1408.

The *most famous* is the game played every year since 1454 in Marostica, Italy. The castles are played by two soldiers, and the knights are mounted on horses.

In the Moscow Sport Palace in 1962 two World Champions played each other at living chess, with ballet dancers for pieces. M. M. Botwinnik and V. Smyslov drew.

In the slowest game on record – there was no time-limit – Capablanca and Sir G. Thomas played for so long (in Margate) that the queen's rook's pawn fainted. No one moved her once, in the whole game.

## GAMES

**Cards.** The tallest house of cards was sixty-one cards high, 3·53 m (11 ft 7 ins.), made of 3,650 cards, by James Warnock of Canada. An Englishman, Joe E. Whitlam, built one, seventy-three cards high, 13 ft 10¼ ins. (4·2 m), but he bent some of the cards, to help support it.

**Ducks and Drakes.** The record is twenty-four skips (ten *plinkers* and 14 *pittypats*).

**Dominoes.** Michael Cairney of New York spent *thirteen days* setting up 169,713 dominoes covering 6·9 km (4·3 miles). He gave one a push, and they all fell over, one after the other in under 2 hrs.

**Lego.** Legoland at Billund in Denmark covers 15 acres with model towns and buildings, using 12 million bricks. The Dutch queen's castle, Amalienborg, uses 900,000; a monument of four U.S. presidents' heads, much larger than life-size, uses 1·5 million.

**Musical chairs.** 3,729 people played musical chairs at Butlin's in Filey, Yorkshire, on 20 July 1978.

**Skipping.** Katsumi Suzuki of Japan is the only person to have turned a skipping rope five times in one jump.

**Boomerangs.** Herb Smith of Ford, Arundel, Sussex, holds the world record for boomerang-throwing; a distance of 105·5 m (346 ft) before the boomerang turns and comes back again. He makes all his own boomerangs, usually out of birch ply, but they can be made out of anything, even plastic or aluminium. Early boomerangs were made from naturally bent sticks and date from the time of Tutankhamun
in the 14th century BC.

**Swinging.** Mollie Jackson of Tarrytown, New York, has swung continuously for 185 hrs.

## TEDDY BEARS AND DOLLS

**First.** The first Teddy Bear was made in 1902, and this is how he got his name. Teddy Roosevelt, the President of the U.S.A., while out bear-hunting in 1902, saved a little bear cub. The newspapers called it 'Teddy's Bear'. Morris Michtom, who ran a stationery shop, cut out a small bear in stuffed brown plush and put it in his window. Twelve passers-by asked for a copy. Mr Michtom made more and wrote to the President, asking if he could call it The Teddy Bear. The President replied: 'Dear Mr Michtom, I don't think my name is likely to be worth much in the bear business, but you are welcome to use it.' He was wrong about that: Mr Michtom made thousands of bears after that, and so have lots of other people.

**Largest.** The biggest jointed teddy bear is 9 ft 4 ins. (3·6 m) (made by Chad Valley).

**Collections.** Mr Matt Murphy of San Francisco, U.S.A., has the largest collection of bears – 1,155 in December 1979. The biggest collection in Britain, and possibly Europe, belongs to Col. Robert Henderson of Edinburgh – 471 bears.

**Fastest.** Mr Woppit, speed king Donald Campbell's bear, travelled with him in *Bluebird* at 328 m.p.h. on water, and in all his record-breaking land-speed runs.

**Hand-made.** Mrs Helen Henderson of Canada has made over 19,000 bears by hand.

**Parachuting.** Senior Under Officer Edward Bear, of the Royal Military Academy, Sandhurst, has made over 300 parachute descents, with his own parachute and dressed in the uniform of an officer cadet.

**Highest.** Mishka, the black and white teddy mascot for the 1980 Olympic games, visited space aboard the *Salyut 6* orbiting station in 1979, to become the world's first ever Space Teddy.

**Mountaineer.** Zissi climbed the Matterhorn, one of the highest mountains in Europe, with his owner, Walter Bonnati, in 1965, and saved his life. Bonnati was caught in a storm, had to spend the night on the mountain and talked to Zissi all night, preventing himself from panicking and falling to his death.

**Most travelled.** Sir Edward Bear was found alone on an empty plane in Sydney, Australia, on 21 June 1975. From then on he travelled the world by plane, looking for his owner, with his own log book. Customs inspectors stamped the book but because he was a 'non-person', he was not allowed to land. Finally, on 7 September 1975 he was reunited with his owner, Jamie Fowler, aged 4, at Los Angeles International Airport, after an estimated 150,000 miles by air and more than 300 flying hours.

**Free pass.** Benny, a 5-year-old bear, was given a free pass on 850 Tyneside buses 'for the rest of his life', in September 1979. Benny is owned by Laura Ashley, aged 12.

**Good Bears of the World.** The Good Bears of the World Association was founded in 1970 by James T. Ownby, with headquarters in Honolulu, U.S.A., for world-wide *arctophiles* (bear lovers). The British branch is run by Colonel Robert Henderson, 17 Barnton

Gardens, Edinburgh. The Association has given approximately 60,000 bears to children in hospitals all over the world.

**Smallest.** The smallest bear in the world is owned by Peter Bull. Tiny is half an inch high and lives on a velvet cushion inside a jewel box.

The smallest *jointed* teddy, which could move its arms, legs and head, was 2½ ins. high. This tiny teddy was banned in 1974 – for being dangerous.

**Teddy Bear Rally.** The world's first Great Teddy Bear Rally was held at Longleat House, Wiltshire, on 27 May 1979. About 2,000 bears and 8,000 people attended. There were marmalade sandwiches and honey cakes for the bears, and 3,000 gingerbread bears for the humans. All the bears were there for a Teddy Bear's Picnic and a Honey Fair: Winnie-the-Pooh, Paddington, Rupert, the largest bear in the world and bears from far away, like Florida and Australia.

**Dolls.** The *oldest British* doll still existing was made in the reign of Henry VIII. In 1548 it was left in her will by the owner to all her descendants and is now in the Leeds Museum. It's got a wooden head covered with plaster and is dressed in red velvet.

The *oldest doll in the world* is probably a painted wooden doll with movable arms and a short white dress, found in the tomb of a Pharaoh's daughter in Thebes, Egypt, and put there about 1200 BC.

The first *talking* dolls were made in 1830, *shut-eye* dolls in 1826 and an *eating* doll in 1880; she ate a sweet and it came out at the bottom of her foot! The Dy-Dee Doll was the first doll to drink water, and then, a few minutes later, wet its nappy.

**Titania's Palace.** The most expensive doll's house ever sold is the magnificent Titania's Palace, which fetched a record £148,500 at an auction in 1978. (Bought by the Lego Museum.)

It was made for a little girl called Gwendolen Wilkinson. They started building it when she was 3 years old, but it was so carefully built and grew so big and elaborate with so many marvellous pieces of furniture in it, that Gwendolen grew faster than her Palace and she was grown-up by the time it was finished.

The Palace is 12 ft by 8 ft and 6 ft high and built round a courtyard. In the courtyard there is a fountain made of gold, diamonds and enamel. An elegant dome on the roof contains a musical box, playing tunes. It has an entrance hall, called the Hall of the Fairy Kiss, a Throne Room, two State Rooms, a chapel, four other reception rooms, five bedrooms, a nursery, and a bathroom with a dark green marble bath. The nursery is filled with tiny toys, all made to scale, including a little silver copy of the Palace itself. Every room is filled with valuable carpets, pictures and objects, and the whole Palace contains about 2,000 pieces of miniature furniture. The Palace has no doors, because it is a Fairy Palace, and Oberon and Titania and the other fairy people don't need them.

# Amazing Animals

## CATS

**Oldest puss.** 'Puss', owned by Mrs Holway, of Clay-hidon, Devon, lived for a record thirty-six years and one day.

**Most travelled.** A Siamese cat called Lucky escaped from her box in a Boeing 747 on 9 October 1979. For the next thirty-two days the plane circled the globe and flew to nearly every country. Lucky was found, crouched in the hold and just alive, when the plane landed at Heathrow on 12 November 1979.

**Climbing kitten.** In September 1950, a 4-month-old black and white kitten left the Hotel Belvedere (10,820 ft or 3,298 m) in the Swiss Alps, and began climbing the Matterhorn, one of Europe's highest mountains. Two mornings later, climbers found him at the summit

(14,780 ft or 4,505 m), meowing and tail-in-air. They shared their meal with him and brought him down.

**Kindest.** Sir Henry Wyatt, a 15th-century nobleman, was sent to the Tower of London and condemned to die of starvation. But luckily his cat followed him and brought him a pigeon every day down the chimney. The gaoler cooked it; Sir Henry ate it, survived, and was later released.

**Long-distance.** Rusty, a ginger tom, followed his owner 950 miles from Boston to Chicago, Illinois, U.S.A., in 1949. It took him eighty-three days.

**Tree-sitting.** A cat called Mincha ran up a tree in Buenos Aires, South America, and stayed there for six years. She had three lots of kittens up among the branches.

**Cat-lover.** Mohammed was said to have taken a pair of scissors and cut away the hem of his cloak before standing up, rather than disturb a sleeping cat.

**Flying cat.** Windy belonged to Wing-Commander Guy Gibson, V.C., leader of the famous Dambusters. In World War II Windy went flying whenever Wing-Commander Gibson flew, putting in 'more flying hours than most cats'.

**Richest cats.** A pair of cats inherited the entire estate of their owner, a California doctor, in 1963 – $415,000 (about £200,000).

# DOGS

**Oldest.** Bluey, a Queensland cattle and sheep dog, lived for twenty-nine years five months, most of that time as a working dog.

**Largest litters.** Twenty-three foxhound pups – born in Ambler, Pennsylvania, U.S.A., in June 1944.

**Strangest litter.** In December 1972, a Great Dane, who had mated with a dachshund produced thirteen Great Little Danehunds and Little Great Dachsdanes.

**Rarest.** The rarest dogs are the Tahl-Tan bear dogs. There are only three of them, and they all live in Canada.

**Long-distance.** Bobbie – a collie – was lost by his owners while on holiday in Wolcott, Indiana, U.S.A. Six months later he came home to Silverton, Oregon, having crossed the Rocky Mountains in winter time and walked about 2,000 miles.

A fox terrier, lost in Hayes Creek, Australia, found his way home to Mambray Creek, 1,700 desert miles away.

**Mountain.** Barry, the St Bernard mountain rescue dog, saved forty travellers lost in blizzards in twelve years. (The 41st, unfortunately, thought he was a bear, and killed him with an ice-axe.) His body has been kept and Barry can still be seen in the National Museum, Berne, Switzerland.

**Dog king.** His Royal Highness Suening the Dog ruled Norway for three years in the 11th century – and this is how it came about.

The King before – King Eystein – had been hounded out of the country. When he eventually got back, he said to his people: 'Very well. If you don't really want me, which would you rather have instead – a dog or a slave?' They said, 'A dog, please.' So Suening the dog was put on the throne, with a court, counsellors, guard and officers to attend him. They said he could distinctly speak two Norwegian words and bark one more. He reigned for three years, signing decrees and orders with his paw-mark, and when he died (saving a lamb from a wolf) they gave him a state funeral.

**Heart transplant.** A dog in America has lived for three years with a transplanted heart.

**Dog-basket.** The strangest dog-basket belonged to Henry III of England. The King was so mad about dogs that he used to turn up to Royal Councils with a small basket round his neck, trimmed with ribbons and full of little dogs. (They were Papillons, a kind of miniature French spaniel.)

**Dog-in-boots.** A dog called Free Fall – his other hobby is parachuting – ran 1,380 miles from top to bottom of New Zealand with his master, Major Albert Kiwi, in 1978. He wore lace-up leather boots to protect his poor paws.

**Most dogs.** U.S.A. has an estimated 41 million dogs. 25,000 dogs are born every day, and about 1 million stray dogs live in New York. The most popular dog in the U.S.A. is the poodle – one in five pedigree dogs is a poodle.

## MOST FAITHFUL DOGS

**Boatswain.** The highest praise ever recorded for a dog, is found on the tombstone of Lord Byron's dog, Boatswain, at Newstead Abbey, England. It reads:
Near this spot are deposited the remains of one
Who possessed Beauty without Vanity,
Strength without Insolence,

Courage without Ferocity
and all the Virtues of Man without his Vices.
This praise, which would be unmeaning Flattery
if inscribed over human ashes,
is but a just tribute to the Memory of
BOATSWAIN, a Dog born in Newfoundland, May 1803.
Died at Newstead Abbey, 18th November 1808.

**Hachiko.** Every day, Hachiko, a Chow Chow dog
living in Tokyo, Japan, went with his master to the
station in the morning and met him again in the evening. One evening in 1925, his master did not return.(He
had died of a stroke.) But Hachiko continued to wait
for him at the station. He waited for ten years, until he
too died – in 1935. The Japanese honoured his loyalty
with a memorial and put Hachiko's portrait on a postage stamp.

**Greyfriars Bobby.** The most famous dog memorial
in Scotland is that of Greyfriars Bobby, the little Skye
terrier – in Princes Street Gardens, Edinburgh.

Bobby the terrier used to go every day to a café in
Edinburgh, where his master had a cup of tea and he
had a bun. One day his master died. Next day, Bobby
turned up at the café as usual – was given his bun, and
left. After several days, when the same thing had
happened, the café owner followed Bobby out and
found that he spent the rest of the day sitting on his
master's grave. The faithful dog kept his lonely vigil
at the grave for the next fourteen years. When Bobby
died, the statue was put up in his memory.

**Carraya.** Carraya was a mongrel dog, belonging to a Spanish shepherd. Unfortunately she occasionally bit the sheep, so her owner threw her into an underground cave in the mountains, thinking that was an end of her. But Carraya survived, having fallen on the side of a subterranean lake 200 ft down. Three years later she was found, after living for all that time alone in the darkness, feeding on sheep and pigs who had fallen down into her pit. When she came out, she was dazzled by the light. *Then she ran over to her master and licked his hand.*


# REMOTE-CONTROL COLLIES
# AND OTHER UNUSUAL ANIMALS

**Car mirrors.** Rollo, the Pyrenean mountain dog, of Bodmin, Cornwall, holds the record (human *and* dog) for biting off car wing mirrors – seventeen up to the end of 1979, including two off police cars. (*Not* a wise move.)

**Remote-control collie.** Freda, the collie, of Tunbridge Wells, Kent, is the only dog known who can adjust the telly by scratching or shaking her head. When she does, the sound goes up and down. It's happened ever since the TV control unit got lost.

**Vet chimp.** The only chimpanzee vet's assistant lives and works in Japan; wears a mob cap and apron; helps carry dogs about; holds canaries; and sits down to a well-earned dinner of bananas and cabbages after work with his boss, the vet.

**Water-skiing squirrel.** Twiggy is the world's only known water-skiing squirrel. She trains on peanut butter, grips the skis with her forepaws and gets towed round the lake at Sandford, Florida, U.S.A., by a remote-controlled powerboat at 12 m.p.h.

**Larry the llama.** Larry the llama is the only llama on record who does the weekly shopping in Britain. Miss Julie Cook rides him into Pickering, North Yorkshire, and Larry carries the groceries home.

**Railway baboon.** The cleverest baboon on record was a chacma baboon called Jack. He belonged to James Wide, a signalman in South Africa. Mr Wide had lost both legs, so Jack pushed him to work each day in his wheelchair. Then he learned to operate the signal levers and worked as a signalman's assistant for nine years. He died in 1890.

**Boxing kangaroo.** Fuji the kangaroo, a circus boxer from Tokyo, is the only kangaroo known to have laid out three policemen. It happened like this ... Fuji escaped from his trainer on 21 July 1966, with his boxing gloves still on, and dashed out into the streets. Several police cars chased him at speeds up to 40 m.p.h. But they caught him, and that's when Fuji floored the three policemen, with a quick right, left and right again to the body. After that, someone put a judo submission hold on him.

**Minnie the Moo.** The smallest cow in the world is 32 ins. high and belongs to Cecil Newton, a Lincolnshire farmer. Her name is Minnie the Moo.

**Golden oldie.** 'Goldie', a goldfish belonging to Mr Taylor of Sleaford, Lincolnshire, lived for a record thirty-six years.

**Golden hamsters.** The largest litter of hamsters on record is a litter of eighteen golden hamsters. All the golden hamsters in England are descended from just one litter, caught in Syria in 1930.

**Hamster farm.** The only hamster farm in Britain is owned by Percy Parslow at Great Bookham, Surrey. He breeds 118 champion varieties, including cinnamons, honeys, chocolates, satins, mosaics, long hairs, sepias, piebalds, tortoiseshells, blonds and pinks. A satinized tortoiseshell and white costs £300. About 250 baby hamsters are born there every day.

**Bionic poodle.** When Ubu, a 6-year-old poodle, hurt his Achilles tendon very badly, it was feared he would have to be put down. But in September 1979, surgeons threaded carbon fibre through his leg and made such an amazingly strong, springy, bouncy, powerful leg, it was positively bionic.

**Oldest mouse.** The oldest pet mouse was called Hercules. He lived in Surrey to a record 5 years and 11 months. But in 1978, a colony of 6-year-old mice were put on show in London. They had been deep-frozen as embryos for five and a half years and *then* they had their first birthday.

**Most talkative bird.** Prudle, a male grey African parrot, holds the world record for talking, with a vocabulary of nearly 1,000 words. He won the best-talking parrot title in London from 1965 to 1976 and retired in 1977 to talk in private.

A budgerigar called Sparkie Williams was the world's most chatty budgie. He could say 531 words, including 'budgerigar' and 'chatterbox'. He lived to be 8 years old and his last words were: 'I love Mama.'

## HORSES

**Fastest.** The fastest speed for a horse is 43·26 m.p.h. Big Racket, a Mexican horse, set the record over a $\frac{1}{4}$-mile in Mexico in 1945, and it hasn't been beaten yet.

**Smallest.** The tiniest real horses are the Fallabella horses, bred in Argentina. The smallest of them are only 40 cm (16 ins.) tall.

**Highest jump.** A world record height – 8 ft 6 ins. (2·6 m) – was jumped by Jack Martin on a horse called Gold Meade in Cairns, Australia, 1946.

**First steeplechase.** The first steeplechase took place in Co. Cork, Ireland, in 1752. Two Irishmen called O'Callaghan and Blake raced against each other across country from Buttevant Church to within sight of the St Leger church *steeple* – 4½ miles away.

**Red Rum.** Red Rum is the only horse to win the Grand National three times – in 1973, 1974 and 1977. He only ran in the race five times – he came second in 1975 and 1976.

**Smoothest ride.** The Tennessee Walking Horse can canter so smoothly that a glass of water balanced on its quarters will not spill a drop.

# DINOSAURS

**Longest.** *Diplodocus* was $87\frac{1}{2}$ ft (27 m) long – nearly as long as three London double-decker buses. You can see him in the Carnegie Museum, Pittsburgh, Pennsylvania, U.S.A.

**Heaviest.** *Brachiosaurus brancai.* You can see his bones in the Museum für Naturkunde, East Berlin, Germany. With all his flesh on his old bones he would have weighed 77 tons.

**Smallest.** The bones of a young dinosaur (*Psittacosaurus mongoliensis*) with a beak like a parrot were found in Mongolia in 1980. It was only 10 ins. long – the size of this open book, and the smallest dinosaur known to science. As its teeth were worn, it wasn't even newly hatched, so when this mini-dinosaur first stepped out of its egg it must have been even smaller, and the tiniest little pipsqueak parrot-beak, compared to his Mum and Dad who were over 6 ft long.

**Nut-brain.** The *Stegosaurus*, a hunch-backed dinosaur with big spines down its back and 30 ft long, had a brain the size of a walnut – weighing $\frac{1}{20}$th of a human brain.

**Absent/Missing.** *Supersaurus* – or, at least, some of his neckbones – was discovered in 1972, in Colorado, U.S.A. They are still looking for the rest of him or her, but people think he must have been about 130 ft long, 75 ft high with his/her head up and about 250 tons in weight.

If they're proved right, then *Supersaurus* is the world's greatest ever SUPERBEAST.

## MOST VENOMOUS ANIMALS

**Snakes.** Front-fanged snakes – cobras, mambas and the king cobra, which can grow to 6 m long – are the deadliest. Their venom is so deadly that 1 g can kill 150 people. Just to handle the substance can put you into a coma.

**Fish.** The stonefish is the most dangerous of all venomous fish. It is very ugly too. It looks just like a very old rock, encrusted with barnacles, until it opens its enormous mouth. It has thirteen spines, loaded with poison, on its back, which rise up when danger threatens, and these can penetrate a thick rubber sole. The pain is said to be worse than any other animal poison and can cause death.

**Spiders.** The deadliest spider is the *Atrax robustus*, a tunnel-web spider, which lives in the Sydney area of Australia. The spider makes two neat punctures in your skin, which look like a snake-bite. No antidote serum has yet been found. The venom of the male is six times more poisonous than the female's.

**Jellyfish.** The seawasp is the most venomous jellyfish. It lies off the coast of Queensland in Australia and on the Great Barrier Reef. Between 1945 and 1970, sixty people died of a seawasp sting, within minutes of being stung. (Man-eating sharks only killed thirteen people.)

**Frogs.** The South American tree-frog, *Phyllobates*, secretes from its skin one of the strongest poisons known. It is used by Indians to tip their poison arrows. The tiniest drop in a wound is enough to kill a man.

# THE MOST MYSTERIOUS
# FOOTPRINTS

**The Sasquatch or Bigfoot** is a big hairy creature who lives in the north-west states of America, and west Canada. The only film ever taken of him was shot by Roger Patterson, while on a Sasquatch hunt at Bluff Creek, northern California, on 20 October 1967. The pictures show a hairy, man-like creature, walking upright, about 100 ft from the camera.

In May 1974, Jack Cochran, a logger, saw a 'big, hairy thing' standing silently about 50 yds away in the Hood River National Forest in Oregon, U.S.A. It walked away, on two legs, leaving only its footprints as a record.

Many plaster casts of his enormous tracks have been made. In 1969, he left a half-mile trail of 1,089 foot-

prints, near Bossburgh in Washington State. The prints were $17\frac{1}{2}$ ins. long and 7 ins. wide.

**The Yeti or Abominable Snowman** has left his colossal and strange footprints in the snow high up in the Himalayan Mountains. The British mountaineer, Eric Shipton, saw them at a height of 18,000 ft. From the footprints, which continued for about a mile and then disappeared on some ice, he reckoned the creature must have been about 8 ft tall.

The yeti was seen by Don Whillans, a climber, in the summer of 1970 at a height of 13,000 ft in Nepal. He spent the day photographing some very large unknown tracks in the snow; that night, in the moonlight, he saw an ape-like creature moving along a ridge opposite his tent.

**The Hairy Wild Men** of the Pamir Mountains in Soviet Central Asia have sometimes been glimpsed, but mostly they too just leave their mysterious Bigfoot tracks for explorers to wonder at. A scientist from Leningrad University saw one in 1957. He said it was reddish-grey, hairy and long-armed, with an ungainly, shambling walk.

Several Russian expeditions have found traces of the footprints. In the autumn of 1979, four traces of bare feet with a pace length of 47 ins., twice as long as the average human pace, were found. A plaster cast made of the imprint shows the foot was 13·4 ins. (34 cm) long and 6·3 ins. (16 cm) across the toes. Scientists said the creature was hominoid, like the Sasquatch. The Russians are still searching for the Hairy Man.

# MUMMIES

**The oldest surviving mummy** is a man, Waty, a court musician, who lived about 4,500 years ago. He still lies in his coffin in Nefer's tomb at Saqqara, near Cairo, in Egypt. His body was so cleverly wrapped that you can still see his features, beneath the bandages, down to the tiniest wart and wrinkle.

**Cat mummies.** The biggest hoard of cat mummies – 300,000 altogether – was found near Beni-Hasan, between Cairo and Luxor, in 1859. They were mostly marmalade cats with big ears and long paws. They were put in little bronze coffins or just wrapped in bandages, with their heads covered in a bronze mask with gold eyes. (The Egyptian name for a cat was – *Miu*.)

Thousands of *mice mummies* have been found too. The mice were preserved for the sake of the cats.

# Kids

## YOUNGEST RECORDS

**National title.** Youngest person ever to win a national sports title was Joy Foster, aged 8, who won the Jamaican singles and mixed doubles championships for table tennis in 1958.

**Colonel.** The son of ex-President Somoza of Nicaragua was made a colonel – on full pay – on the day he was born.

**Widow.** The Duke of Buckingham's daughter was a widow when she was 9 years old. (This was several centuries ago.)

**Wife.** Françoise de Lorraine was 3 years old when she became the wife of Henri IV's 4-year-old son.

**Wimbledon.** Youngest Wimbledon champion is Charlotte Dod. She became singles champion in 1887, when she was 15 years 8 months old.

**King.** The youngest King ever known was Sapor II of the House of Sassan, who ruled Persia in the 4th century. He was crowned before he was born. Wise men were so sure his mother, widow of Shah Hormouz, was going to bear a son that they placed a crown on her stomach with the baby king inside and he was crowned inside his mother.

**Grandmother.** Mum-zi, the favourite wife of Chief AkKivi of Calabar in Africa, was a grandmother when she was 17. She had a child when she was 8, and so did her daughter.

**Artist.** Youngest exhibitor at the Royal Academy Summer Exhibition is Lewis Lyons. In 1967, when he was 5 years old, they showed a picture of his called 'Trees and Monkeys'.

**Author.** Dorothy Straight of Washington D.C., U.S.A., wrote *How the World Began* when she was 4. The book was published by Pantheon Books, New York, 1964.

Teresa Walsh, Robert Bridge and Barbara Griffiths, all aged 5, have written stories published in *The Big Desmond Story Book* in 1979 (Dinosaur Publications Ltd, England).

Daisy Ashford was 9 when she wrote the famous and best-selling book, *The Young Visiters*. It was first published in 1919 and is still in print (Chatto & Windus, London).

**Hole-in-one.** Tommy Moore of Hagerstown, Maryland, U.S.A., hit the ball 145 yds, from the tee into the hole, on 8 March 1968, when he was 6 years old.

**Millionaire.** Shirley Temple, the American child film-star, made a million before she was 10 years old. She was a film-star when she was 3 years old.

## THE WORLD'S WILDEST KIDS

**Wolf-children.** The world's wildest kids are *cubs* – children brought up by wolves like wolf-cubs.

*The most famous* are Amala and Kerala, who were found in Orissa, India, living with wolves in 1920. The Rev. Singh, who ran an orphanage, rescued them and took them home. Amala was 1½ and Kerala was about 8.

They had thick skin on their hands, knees and elbows, and ran on their hands and feet, tongues out, panting. In the daytime, they crouched in the shade or stood motionless with their faces to the wall. But at night they came awake; they howled and hunted. They chased chickens and killed them, but they liked dogs and cats. Amala didn't live very long, but Kerala lived for another eight years, and gradually learnt to get on with the other children in the orphanage, wearing clothes – she loved everything red – and even learning to speak a little.

A wolf-boy of about 10 or 11 is now living in a mission near Lucknow in India. His name is Shamdev and he was found playing with wolf-cubs in the forest in 1973. He has got thick skin on his elbows and knees like other wolf-children, and when he smiles he shows very sharp pointed front teeth.

The oldest known wolf-children were the twin brothers, Romulus and Remus, who were looked after by a she-wolf, and later founded the city of Rome in Italy.

**Monkey-boy.** A 6-year-old boy was found living with a herd of monkeys in Burundi, Africa in 1975. The monkeys all scampered up trees, but the boy wasn't quite so fast and got caught. He couldn't speak, walked on all fours and scratched people, but he has now learnt to walk upright and speak a few words.

**The Gazelle-boy of the Spanish Sahara.** In 1961, a Frenchman, exploring the Great Desert of the Rio de Oro in the Spanish Sahara, North-West Africa, saw a young boy, possibly about 10 years old, living with a herd of gazelles. The boy was quite wild and couldn't speak but acted just like a gazelle, leaping and prancing, signalling to the others with his face-muscles and his finger-tips.

The Frenchman observed him for some weeks, watching him scampering along the ground on all fours, climbing date-palms, standing suddenly upright, rigid, and then running and bounding away, keeping up with the other gazelles.

He returned to the desert in 1963 with two army men and a jeep. They followed the boy and the herd of gazelles at a speed of 52–54 km/h but could not catch him. In 1966 some American officers tried but failed to catch him with two helicopters and a net.

The gazelle-boy was never captured and never seen again.

## PRODIGIES

**Highest I.Q.** The highest I.Q. known is 210, for Kim Ung-Yong of Seoul, South Korea, born 7 March 1963. Aged 4 years and 8 months, he could write poetry, speak four languages, Korean, English, German and Japanese, and perform integral calculus, an advanced form of mathematics.

His parents may be record-makers too; they were both born at exactly the same time – 11 a.m. 23 May 1934.

**The girl genius.** Edith Stern, of Brooklyn, New York, U.S.A., has an I.Q. of over 200. When she was born on 16 August 1952, her parents said: 'She's going to be a genius.' So they:

Played classical music in her nursery 24 hrs a day.

Put cards with numbers and animals in her cot.

Put the first volume of the *Encyclopaedia Britannica* in her cot when she was $1\frac{1}{2}$, and the others, volume by volume, until she was 4.

When Edith was 11 months old, her father asked her how old she was – she picked up a card with 10 on it and put up one finger. She had read the whole encyclopaedia by the time she was $4\frac{1}{2}$. She went to school at 6 – skipped secondary school and went to University at 12. She started smoking at that age. She is now very overweight and not tremendously successful, but she *has* got a high I.Q.


## MATHEMATICAL WHIZZ-KIDS

Before everyone learnt to read and write, and before tests and I.Q.s and calculators, a few boys startled the world by their ability to do extraordinary sums *entirely in their heads*. (There is no record of a girl doing the same, but because none has been heard of, it does not necessarily mean they did not exist.) The most famous of these mathematical geniuses are:

**Jedediah Buxton.** Born about 1707, in Elmton, Derbyshire, England. Jedediah worked out (in his *head*) how many cubic inches there were in a right-angled block of stone 23,145,789 yds long, 5,642,732 yds wide and 54,965 yds thick. (36 ins. = 1 yd, in case you want to try.)

When Jedediah was told the exact thickness of a

hair 1 in. long, he calculated how many hairs it would take to fill a cube whose volume was 202,680,000,360 cubic miles.

Jedediah Buxton was a farm-labourer all his life and never learnt to read or write.

**Zerah Colburn.** Born 1804 in Cabut, Vermont, U.S.A., Zerah was especially good at finding factors of numbers. When he was still a young boy, he answered questions like these almost immediately:

What are the factors of 171,395? Answer: 5, 7, 59 and 83.

What is the product of 21,734 and 543? Answer: 11,801,562.

Zerah was sent to Westminster School in London, England, but the more he got educated, the worse he got at working out sums in his head.

**George Parker Bidder.** Born 1806 in Moreton Hampstead in Devon, England. George's father was a stone-mason, and George taught himself to multiply and divide by rearranging marbles and buttons into patterns.

When he was only 10 years old, he was asked: 'What is the square root of 119,550,669,121?' He gave the answer in 30 secs. — 345,761.

When he was 12, he was asked: 'If the pendulum of a clock goes $9\frac{3}{4}$ ins. in a second, how many inches will it vibrate in 7 years, 14 days, 2 hours, 1 minute, 56 seconds, if one year contains 365 days, 5 hours, 48 minutes, 55 seconds?'! George thought for less than one minute and gave the answer – 2,165,625,744¾ ins.

George Bidder went to university and became a civil engineer, but the more he learnt the less good he became at doing mental arithmetic.

(One of George's brothers, by the way, had a most remarkable memory. He knew the whole Bible by heart.)

**Truman Henry Stafford.** Truman, an American boy, was another mathematical genius, and this is what happened when *he* worked out a sum in his head:

'Truman,' they said, 'multiply in your head 365,365,365,365,365,365 by 365,365,365,365,365,365.'

*This* is what happened next: 'Truman flew around the Room like a Top, Pulled his Pantaloons over the tops of his Boots, Bit his Hands, Rolled his Eyes in their Sockets, sometimes Smiling and Talking, then Seeming to be in an Agony, until in not more than one Minute, he replied: "133,491,850,208,566,925,016,658,299,941, 583,225".' Which, as it happens, is the right answer.

# RECORD-MAKING CHILDREN

**Tallest girl.** Ella Ewing, of Missouri, U.S.A., was 6 ft 9 ins. (206 cm) when she was 10 years old.

**Fattest.** The fattest girls in the world live in South-East Nigeria, Africa. When a girl there becomes engaged, she is sent to a fattening centre to get as plump as possible, because a fat, idle wife shows that her father and husband must be wealthy men. The wealthier the father, the longer a girl stays at the centre; the longer she stays, the fatter she gets; the fatter the wife, the more flattered the husband.

The court of the Ugandan kings used to be filled with a harem of the fattest young wives the world has ever seen. They were so fat that they could not stand upright but lay about like seals. Their diet was milk, and if the young wives did not take enough, they were forcibly fed.

**Tallest boy.** Robert Wadlow, U.S.A., was 6 ft 10½ ins. (2·1 m) when he was 12 years old.

**Smallest girl.** Pauline Musters, of Ossendrecht, Holland, was 55 cm tall when she was 9 years old.

**Smallest boy.** Jozef Boruwalaski (born in Poland in 1739) was 53 cm tall when he was 10 years old. He grew another 9 cm in the next five years.

**Third eye.** It was reported in 1976 that a 10-year-old Japanese girl, Sayuri Tanaka, can see with her nose. She can read, cycle, score at basket-ball and watch television blindfold. She can see through a part of the left side of her nose just as well as with her eyes.

**Bravest.** On 19 December 1979 ten children received Children of Courage awards, including Roy Gadd, 10, who punched a circus leopard (which was clawing a friend's arm) – WHAM! straight between the eyes.

**The Albert Medal** is a medal for outstanding bravery, for civilians. The winners get £100 a year for life. The youngest medallists are Anthony Fraser, 8, and Dorothy Ashburnum, 11, who saved each other's lives when attacked by a cougar in Canada, and David Western, 10, who tried to save three others, who had fallen through the ice of a frozen lake.

## TWINS

**Siamese.** The first Siamese twins *were* Siamese. Chang and Eng Bunker were born in Thailand, which was called Siam then, in 1811. They were joined at the chest and never parted. One married Sarah Yates and had ten children, the other married her sister Adelaide and had twelve children. They both died on 17 January 1874. .

**Twin-talk.** Grace and Virginia are identical twins, who live in California. They call each other *Poto* and

*Cabenga*, and until they were 7 in 1978, they only spoke their own language, which sounds like this:

'*Cabenga, padem manibadu peeta*,' says Grace.

'*Doan nee bada tengkmatt, Poto*,' says Virginia.

They can understand English, but can only speak it a little. They lived most of the time with their German grandmother, who didn't say much, so they just made up their own language and chattered away, incredibly fast. Doctors in San Diego are making tapes of it and trying to work it out – but it's not easy.

When Grace says to Virginia, '*Snap, aduk, Cabenga, chase die-dipana*,' they both go and play with their doll's house!

**Identical.** Ninety-six sets of identical twins, identically dressed, disembarked two by two from the Swedish ferry at Felixstowe on 7 October 1977 – surely the most confusing sight ever seen.

# SCHOOLS

**Smallest.** Soay island school had one pupil, Sarah Maitland, aged 7 in 1978. The island – off the coast of Scotland – has a population of thirteen.

**Largest.** De Witt Clinton High School in the Bronx, New York, had 12,000 pupils in 1934.

**Largest invisible.** The School of the Air, in Alice Springs, Australia, stretches for half a million square miles and has 120 pupils and 13 teachers, who only meet for one week in August. The teaching is done over two-way radio in the Northern Territories, where few people live. The nearest boy or girl in the class could be 1,000 miles away.

**Longest holiday.** The longest school holiday on record lasted from June 1966 to March 1967, when 110 million Chinese children over 9 years old were excused school to take part in the Cultural Revolution. (And probably worked hard at something else.)

**Shortest exam answer.** Winston Churchill sat a Latin exam to get into Harrow School. This is what he managed to do, in his own words: 'I wrote my name at the top of the page. I wrote the number of the question, 1. After much reflection, I put a bracket round it thus (1).' That's all he wrote. But he did get into Harrow, and he did become Prime Minister of England and *Sir* Winston Churchill.

**Cleverest failure.** The greatest physicist of this century, Albert Einstein, failed the entrance examinations to the Federal Polytechnic of Zurich when he was 16.

**Most international.** Hallfield Infants' School in London is the most international state primary school in England. It has pupils from fifty-one countries: Algeria, Argentina, Australia, Bangladesh, Belgium, Bulgaria, Barbados, Brazil, Czechoslovakia, Cyprus, Dominica, Egypt, France, Ghana, Germany, Greece, Hong Kong, Holland (take a breath), India, Iran, Israel, Italy, Jamaica, Kenya, Liberia, Lebanon,

Malaysia, Mexico, Morocco, Mauritius, New Zealand, Nigeria, Nepal, Pakistan, Portugal, Poland (have another), the Philippines, Russia, South Africa, Spain, South Yemen, Sudan, Singapore, Sri Lanka, Turkey, Tunisia, the United Kingdom, Uganda, St Kitts, Yugoslavia and U.S.A. Hardly any of them can speak English when they go there, but it doesn't seem to matter.

**Hardest-working pupils.** Japanese children have to be the hardest working, to win places at the best high schools and universities. A school-day for a Japanese child living on the outskirts of Tokyo goes like this:

4.30 a.m. Get up. Travel to special private lessons (called *Juku*).

8 a.m. Ordinary school begins.

After school, travel to more private lessons. 2-hr journey home, after that.

11 p.m. Homework finished. Go to bed.

**First school sit-in.** At the end of term, in English schools in the 13th century, the Master would be thrown out of the school, the doors locked and the windows barricaded.

If the Master got back in, he punished the children. If they kept him out for three days, then he had to surrender, ask forgiveness and promise to be a better Master in the future.

**Meanest headmaster.** There's lots of competition for this title, but it's safer to mention *dead* headmasters. Two outstanding candidates are . . .

1. Mr Heath, headmaster of Eton many years ago. If ever the Eton College cricket team lost a match, he flogged them all, *including the scorer*.

2. The headmaster of Sherborne College in 1587. He attended all school matches, running round the touch line, screaming in English, Greek and Latin. If he found any boy had enough breath left to speak at the end of a match, he said: 'You haven't tried hard enough' – and beat him.

**First Prep school in Britain.** The Rev. Dr Pearson started a school at Temple Grove, Richmond, London. Pupils began the day with two large spoonfuls of sulphur and treacle. One hour's lessons – then breakfast of watered milk and dry bread. School dinner *began* with rice pudding – to save the meat bill. Pupils never had a bath. On Saturday nights they washed their feet in one tub – six at a time. *The water was never changed.*

**School reports and exams.** Exams are first mentioned by the Head of Shrewsbury School in 1818. Marks were simply – *V* (very good) *W* (well) *w* (pretty well) *t* (tolerable) *i* (idle) *b* (bad).

One American school today gives reports for children to take home to their parents *every single day*.

**Chinese assembly.** Chinese assembly is different from any other school assembly in the world. Chinese schools have their own production units like little factories. One third of all lesson-time is spent working on *assembly lines* – packing brushes, assembling accumulators or making torches and wax crayons.

# Freaky Families

## PARENTS
## AND OTHER PECULIARITIES

**Oldest father.** It has been reported that Neils Paulsen of Upsala, Sweden, died in 1907 at the age of 160, leaving two sons, one aged 9 and the other 103. (This is the world's most impossible record – but it sounds great.)

**Oldest mother.** Mrs Ruth Kistler, of Los Angeles, California, U.S.A., gave birth to Suzan on 18 October 1956, when she was 57 years old.

**Most wives.** King Mongut of Siam – the original King of the musical *The King and I* – had 9,000 wives and concubines.

**Most children.** Mulai Ismail, ruler of Morocco and husband of very many wives, died in 1727, leaving 546 sons and 340 daughters.

The first wife of Fyodor Vassilet, a Russian peasant, had sixty-nine children – sixteen pairs of twins, seven sets of triplets and four sets of quadruplets. There is no record of how many children Fyodor's *second* wife had.

**Holy Father.** The last Pope to be a father was Rodrigo Borgia. He had at least four children before he became Pope Alexander VI in 1492.

**Grandfather.** Thompson Horan of Gosforth, New-castle, made twelve short hang-gliding flights in 1980, before his instructor grounded him for being too old. Mr Horan is a grandfather of 89.


# BABIES

**Birthdays.** All three Mckay children of Grand Junction, Colorado, U.S.A., have the same birthday. They were born on 11 November 1973, 1975 and 1977.

The most popular time to be born is between 3 and 5 a.m.

**Smallest.** The smallest baby to survive and grow up fit and fine was Marion Chapman, 5 June 1938, in South Shields, County Durham. She was $12\frac{1}{2}$ ins. long and weighed 10 oz. The doctor fed her every hour with a fountain-pen filler.

**Heaviest.** The biggest baby ever born was a boy weighing 11 kg (24 lb. 4 oz.). He was born on 3 June 1961, son of Mrs Saadet Cor of Turkey.

Babies born in May are said to be 200 grams heavier on average than in any other month.

**Toothiest.** A boy was born in Pittsburgh, Pennsylvania, U.S.A., in 1957 with eight teeth. They took them out when he was 3 days old, in case they got loose and stuck in his throat.

**Hairiest.** A Chinese boy was born in 1978 in the province of Liaoning with thick hair all over his body, except for parts of his face, hands and the soles of his feet. His parents called him *Chen Huan* (*Zhenyuan*) – meaning Shock the Universe. Since his birth, thirty-two other hairy babies in ten provinces have been found, but their names aren't known.

**Battle baby.** A boy was born on board *H.M.S. Tremendous*, during the battle of The Glorious First of June, 1794. He was awarded the Naval General

Service medal at birth and named Daniel Tremendous Mackenzie.

**Mini baby.** Josephine-Anne Westlake was born on the front seat of a Mini on 18 September 1979.

**Sextuplets.** David, Nicolette, Jason, Emma, Grant and Elizabeth Rosenkowitz are the world's only surviving sextuplets (born in Cape Town, South Africa, 11 January 1974).

**Quins.** There are three sets of quins in Britain – the Letts quins and the Hanson quins, born in 1969, and the Bostock quins, who are Scottish and were born in 1972.

**Highest.** Baby born on a Dan-Air flight from Tenerife to Manchester, at a height of 25,000 ft.

# WEDDINGS

**Biggest.** On 14 February 1975 Sun Myung Moon married 1,800 couples in one mass wedding. It happened in Seoul, South Korea.

**Quietest.** In 1976 a secretary from Los Angeles, California, U.S.A., called Jannene Swift, married a really strong and silent husband. He was a rock! It was an official wedding, witnessed by more than twenty people. (It was a quiet wedding, though.)

'Do you, Jannene, take this rock to be your lawful wedded husband . . .?'

'I do.'

'Do you – er – Rock, take Jannene to be your lawful wedded wife . . . ?'

. . .

He didn't say Yes, but then he didn't say No, so they were married and lived silently ever after.

**Topless.** Anne Bowman, a topless dancer, was married to Wayne Bray in the Jolly Trolly Casino, in Las Vegas, Nevada, U.S.A., in January 1979. *She* was dressed in a full-length gown, but her fourteen bridesmaids wore only red tights and red top-hats. The ceremony was performed by the Rev. Al Alouf, known as 'Marrying Sam'.

**Trapeze.** Dan Martinez and Lucy Fanfan – both trapeze artists – were married in a circus big top in Oklahoma City, U.S.A., before a congregation, or audience, of 5,000 people. The ceremony was performed by Bishop Ezra Nero of the Landmark Spiritual Temple, suspended 75 ft above the congregation. The wedding couple were higher up – swinging back and forth on their trapezes, as they shouted their vows to each other.

## THE WORLD'S WEIRDEST, STRANGEST, LONGEST, NUTTIEST NAMES

**Greediest.** Susan Eatwell Burpit and Anna Dumpling Cheesecake.

**Most painful.** Mary Cutter Botorff.

**Most unsuitable.** B. A. Gentleman (a lady).

**Gloomiest.** John Will Fail.

**Most hopeful.** Diana May Grow.

**Horsiest.** Adeline Horsey de Horsey.

**Most XYZs.** Mr Zzyzzy Zzyryxxy of Chicago.

**The Z family.** Mr Zuriel Cook of New York had twelve children . . . Zerena, Zuriel, Zerema, Zephrona, Zetna, Zustis, Zelora, Zethaneal, Zeruth, Zelotus, Zedelia and Zejames.

**Number names.** *Mr Ten Million* lived in Seattle, Washington, U.S.A.

*5/8 Smith* lived in Homerville, Georgia, U.S.A.

An English family called Stickney named their three sons *One*, *Two* and *Three* and their three daughters *First*, *Second* and *Third*.

**The latest Marlon Brando.** Mr Adrian Patrick McCarron paid £10 in 1979 to change his name to Marlon Brando. His wife is now Mrs Brando and his five children little Brandos. One of his boys is now Errol Flynn Brando.

**Most confusing.** The 6th Earl FitzWilliam called all his eight boys William. William was the eldest, then there was William, and William and William and William and William, next was William, and finally little William FitzWilliam.

**Commonest.** At least 75 million people are Mr, Mrs, Miss or Master *Chang*.

*Mohammed* is the commonest first name in the world.

The commonest surname in the English-speaking

world is *Smith*. There are more than 2¼ million Smiths in the U.S.A.

From AD 1600 to 1800, half the girls in England were called *Anne*, *Elizabeth* or *Mary*.

**Longest.** The longest surname in Britain belonged to Major L.S.D.O.F. Tollemache-Tollemache de Orellana Plantagenet Tollemache Tollemache.

*The longest name in the world* belonged to Mr Wolfe + 585, Senior, of Pennsylvania, U.S.A. His surname used to have 590 letters, but signing his name became such hard work, he decided to shorten it.

*Name for a lake* – Lake Chargoggagoggmanchau-gagoggchaubunagungamaug in Connecticut, U.S.A. That means, 'You fish on your side, I fish on my side, nobody shall fish in the middle.'

*Swear word* – longest single word on record is the German – *Himmelherrgottkreuzmillionendonnerwetter!* That means, roughly, 'Oh God, for Heaven's sake and a million blooming thunderstorms!'

**Alphabet.** Arthur Pepper of Liverpool christened his daughter – Anna Bertha Cecilia Diana Emily Fanny Gertrude Hypatia Inex Jane Kate Louise Maud Nora Ophelia Prudence Quince Rebecca Sarah Teresa Ulysis Venus Winifred Xenophon Yetty Zeno Pepper.

She was called Alphabet Pepper for short.

**Nicknames.** King William IV of England was the first 'Silly Billy'.

A famous Greek philosopher, called Aristocles, was nicknamed *Plato* by his teacher – which means *Fatty*.

**The backward hills.** Four hills on the Island of Lemnos in the Aegean Sea are called Yam, Yrroc, Eb and Denmad. They were named by some naval men; their commanding officer was called *Corry*. They got away with it, because nobody noticed at first what the letters spelt.

**The craziest names.** The following really existed:

Three American children – Tonsillitis, Meningitis and Appendicitis.

Three Irish children – Joseph, And and Another.

Twins, born in 1887, Queen Victoria's Golden Jubilee year – Jubilhe and Jubilshe.

And *nearly finally* – the baby who was called Finis (meaning The End), but then along came three more babies in the family . . . little Addenda, Appendix and Supplement.

And *finally* – the English girl with nine older brothers and sisters who was called SUFFICIENT.

# Batty Bodies

## BATTY BITS

**Hair on end.** Pierre Massie of Nantes, France, an actor, is the only man on record who could make his hair stand up on end, fall flat or curl. He could make the hair on one side of his head stand up while the other side lay smooth.

**Ear-waggling.** The most famous ear-waggler was the Empress Marie Louise of France, wife of Napoleon I. Not only could she wiggle and waggle them, she could almost turn them inside out. When the Empress felt in the mood for ear-waggling, the Emperor and all his court would rush to her salon to see the show.

**Toothiest ear.** When Mrs Janet Bibby of Higham Ferrers, Northamptonshire, complained of deafness, her doctor syringed her ear, dislodging a little tooth, carefully wrapped in tissue paper. This tooth was probably in her ear from 1949 to 1979 – a record thirty years. Mrs Bibby believes she put it on her pillow when she was 5 years old, hoping the fairies would bring her sixpence, and it lodged in her ear after she fell asleep.

**Hand up.** The fakir, Agastiya, of Bengal, India, held his hand aloft for ten years, from 1902 to 1912, until a little bird built a nest in his palm. His arm was then so rigid that he was never able to put it straight down again.

**Golden nose.** The Swedish astronomer, Tycho Brahe, lost a nose in a duel in 1566. So he had a gold nose made and wore that. It didn't smell too good, but it looked wonderful.

**Rocking teeth.** George Dillard, of Long Island, U.S.A., had great difficulty sleeping in February 1980 – rock music kept on running through his head. He even called the police, he was so desperate about the darn noise. Then he took out his new false teeth. The music stopped. The metal in them had been acting as a radio-receiver for the all-night record programme, 30 miles away.

**Two men, two legs, one pair of shoes.** The *two men* were Americans, Albert Farley and his son. They both lost one leg in accidents, so they had *two legs* between them, one right and one left. They both took the same size shoes, so *one pair of shoes* did for both of them.

**Most bruises.** Lee Asher, aged 10, of Hampshire, England, counted 130 bruises on his body at one time (and he wasn't particularly big).

**Tallest.** The tallest man ever was Robert Wadlow of Alton, Illinois, U.S.A., who died in 1940. He was 272 cm (8 ft 11·1 ins.) tall.

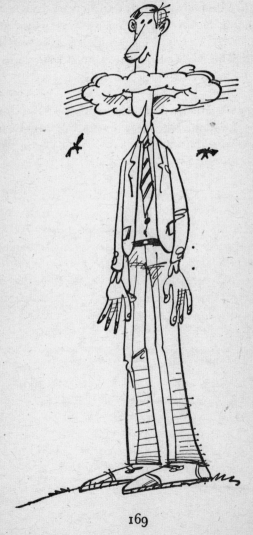

The tallest man in England now is Terence Keenan, of Rock Ferry, Merseyside – 229 cm (7 ft 6 ins.). When he was 17, he was only 163 cm tall.

The tallest living woman is Sandy Allen, of Shelbyville, Indiana, U.S.A. – 231·7 cm (7 ft 7¼ ins.).

**Heaviest.** The heaviest man is Francis John Lang, of Clinton, Iowa, U.S.A., weighing 538 kg.

The heaviest man in Britain is George McAree of Newham, London, who is 179 cm tall and weighs 256 kg.

**Fingers.** The most ever recorded belonged to a baby born in 1938, with fourteen fingers and twelve toes.

The Foldi family, who lived somewhere in Arabia, all had twenty-four fingers and toes.

Anne Boleyn had six fingers on her left hand. She always wore a glove on that hand. She was also reported to have three breasts!

**Huge hands.** Robert Wadlow (the tallest man) had hands 32·5 cm. ($12\frac{3}{4}$ ins.) long.

Nicolo Paganini the violinist had probably the longest hands ever known. His hand span was 18 ins. His long bony fingers were so elastic and bendy at the joints that he could move them equally well in all directions. This helped him to play the violin so amazingly brilliantly that people thought he must be a devil, and no one would bury him in a church graveyard when he died.

**Finger-nails.** A Chinese priest in Shanghai spent twenty-seven years growing his nails to a length of $22\frac{3}{4}$ ins. (58 cm) long.

The longest single finger-nail is $25\frac{1}{2}$ ins. (64·7 cm) long, belonging to Romesh Sharma of Delhi. It took him thirteen years to grow it.

Shridhar Chillal, of Poona, India, has a thumb-nail of 23·2 ins. (59 cm).

(Very long nails like that don't grow straight, they begin to curve and curl round and round like rams' horns.)

**Long necks.** The Paduang women of Burma have the longest necks in the world. They stretch their necks out by gradually putting more and more brass rings round them, until eventually they are 15¾ ins. (40 cm) long.

**Lots of legs.** Frank Lentini, who was born in Sicily in 1889, had three legs, four feet and sixteen toes. He married and had four children and was very good at kicking footballs about.

**Longest moustache.** 2·59 m (8 ft 6 ins.), measured end to end, belonging to Masuriya Din of Uttar Pradesh, India. It must have stretched, each side, to well below his knees.

**Longest beard.** 5·33 m (17½ ft), belonging to Hans N. Langsten of Norway. He went to live in the U.S.A., and how he walked about, I don't know, because his beard would have gone down to his feet, up to his chin, and all the way down again. The beard is now in the Smithsonian Institution in Washington D.C.

Janice Deveree, who was born in Kentucky, U.S.A., in 1842, had a beard 36 cm (14 ins.) long when she was 42.

**Two-toed tribe.** A photograph appeared for the first time in 1980, of a two-toed tribe, living on the borders of Mozambique, Zambia and Botswana in Africa. Each foot divides into two giant claws, ending in a giant toe, like an ostrich. There are probably about ninety people with such feet, though some families have a mixture of five-toed and two-toed children. It's no handicap – in fact the two toes are as good as a hand. The men can pick up a bottle of beer in one foot, a glass in the other and pour themselves a drink.

**The biggest brain.** Brains are not easy to measure – you have to be dead, for one thing, and even then it's not easy. The biggest brains ever measured belonged to Oliver Cromwell, Lord Byron the poet and an anonymous American – all weighing over 4 lb. The average adult brain weighs about 3 lb 1½ oz. Brains get smaller as one gets older!

**The smallest people.** The smallest people in the world are the Onge tribe who live on Little Andaman Island in the Indian Ocean and the Mbuti who live in the forests of the Congo, Africa. Hardly any of them ever grow more than 4 ft 6 ins. (1·4 m) tall.

The most famous little man was called General Tom Thumb. He was born in 1838 in the U.S.A. and was only 102 cm (3 ft 4 ins.) when he died in 1883. He married another little person called Lavinia, and 2,000 guests, including President Lincoln, were at the wedding. In 1978 his waistcoat was sold in London for £60. It measured 8 ins. from neck to waist, and in a pocket was his visiting card, the size of a postage stamp.

**Most tattooed lady.** The most tattooed woman in Britain is Mrs Rusty Skuse of Aldershot, Hampshire. She is a tattooist, and so is her husband, and for thirteen years he has been colouring her in, until now the only untattooed parts of her body are her face, neck, hands and the soles of her feet. He is still working on her, filling in small gaps here and there. He's got much better designs on her now than he had when he first started.

## DEATH-DEFYING BODIES

**The man who didn't own his own body.** In 1890 a Swede sold his body to the Caroline Institute of Stockholm. They gave him cash, and he said they could have his body when he was dead. But then he inherited some money, and said, 'Can I buy my body back, please?' 'No,' said the Institute. 'We made an agreement. Sorry.' And he even had to pay them damages because he'd had two teeth out without their permission!

**The man who killed himself.** Paul Hubert of Bordeaux, France, was convicted of murder in 1863. He served twenty-one years in solitary confinement. Then his case was reopened, and *then* they found he had been convicted of murdering Paul Hubert!

**Dracula.** *Dracula* was written by Bram Stoker in 1897.

Vlad V, ruler of Wallachia in Transylvania, son of Vlad Dracul, is said to be the man who inspired the story. It is true that he was rather a nasty character, having impaled 23,000 people on wooden stakes in his time and liking to watch them writhing while eating his meals, but he wasn't a vampire.

The vampire Bram Stoker probably had in mind was Countess Elizabeth Bathor, who thought she could keep young and beautiful by drinking the blood of young girls. So she had 600 murdered and drained their blood in the dungeons of her Carpathian castles. It did her no good at all. In 1611 she was walled up in her chambers, with a hole for air and food, and was found dead three years later.

# Food

## FANTASTIC FOOD

**Fish and chips.** The first fish and chip shop opened in 1865, in London. Battered fish cost 1d ($\frac{1}{2}$p) a portion.

There are 12,000 shops frying 150,000 tons of fish and 600,000 tons of potatoes in Britain. There's a fish and chip shop in Abu Dhabi, called the Al-Samakeh Al Thahabiya café, selling hammour and chips.

**Fish fingers.** Invented by an American, Mr Birdseye. He called them Fish Sticks. The biggest ever made was $2\frac{1}{2}$ ft long and weighed 60 lb. – more of a fish arm, really.

**Ice-cream.** Marco Polo came back from the East with a recipe for milk-ice in the 13th century.

At Henry V's coronation there was a dessert called *creme frez*, which *sounds* like ice-cream.

**Iced lolly.** The biggest iced lolly weighed 5,750 lb. (2,608 kg) and was made in Davenport, Iowa, U.S.A., in 1975.

*Biggest eaters.* **Americans** eat twice as much ice-cream as any other people – over a billion gallons of ice-cream, ices and sherbet each year, i.e. about 23 quarts per person and enough to fill the Grand Canyon. 100 years ago they ate one teaspoon each.

**Banana split.** The biggest banana split was made for a school fête in Queensland, Australia, in November 1976. It was 1,700 m long, made of 11,333 bananas, 34,000 scoops of ice-cream, 100 gallons of whipped cream, 160 lb. of nuts and 260 gallons of sauce all over it.

**Beefburgers.** The largest was made in Australia in 1975, weighed 2,859 lb. (1,293 kg) and was 8·38 m (26 ft 8 ins.) round.

McDonald's have sold 25 million hamburgers in America – twenty piles as high as the tallest building in the world.

**Hot-dogs.** The biggest hot-dog was made by the German Butchers' Guild in Koenigsberg, Germany. It was half a mile long, weighed 885 lb. (401 kg) and took 103 butchers to carry it.

Americans eat 16 billion frankfurters a year – about 80 for each person.

**Doughnuts.** Doughnuts with a hole in the middle were invented in America as a treat for Shrove Tuesday, Pancake Day in England. They were made with a hole so that children could catch them when their mothers threw the hot doughnuts to them out of the frying-pan.

**The world's biggest sausage.** The colossal sausage was thought up by the Scouts for the biggest children's party in Hyde Park (see below; made by Dewhursts, it was 2 miles long, covered with 267 skins. It was cooked on a 51-ft-long frying-pan, 18 ins. wide. 25,000 portions were stoked, cooked and served by Peter Brooks and lots of cubs and scouts. Prince Philip had a piece and Jamie Cutting (10) had the Queen's piece.

## PARTIES, FEASTS AND BANQUETS

**The biggest children's party.** The party was held in Hyde Park, London, on 30 and 31 May 1979. There were bands, stunt teams, clowns, jugglers, magicians, the Red Devils, dancing, painting, dressing-up and a bubble gum competition. The Queen was there and Prince Philip and Princess Anne. And 160,000 children.

There were 800 loaves of bread to eat, 160,000 bags of crisps, chocolate biscuits and pizzas – 5 tons of yoghurt – a lake of Pepsi. There should have been 20 tons of the world's largest jelly, but there was trouble over the jelling.

**Biggest dish.** Stuffed camel is the world's biggest single dish of food. If you're lucky you might be served it at a Bedouin wedding-feast. First they stuff eggs in fish. Then they stuff the fish inside chickens. Then they stuff chickens inside a sheep. Finally they stuff sheep, chickens, fish and eggs inside a whole camel, and then they have to find a dish big enough to serve it on.

**Biggest banquet.** The biggest banquet on record was held for the new Archbishop of York in 1457. The meat course alone consisted of: 6 wild bulls, 104 oxen, 1,000 sheep, 304 calves, 400 swans, 1,000 capons, 2,000 pigs, 104 peacocks and 13,000 other birds, all washed down with 302,000 old gallons of ale, and 100,800 old gallons of wine. There is no record of how many people stuffed all that inside them.

**Longest feast.** The Old Testament records that Ahasuerus held a feast which went on for 160 days.

## REVOLTING FOOD

**Disgusting eater.** The most revolting eater of all time must be Dr Frank Buckland, a natural historian who lived in Oxford in the 19th century. It was quite usual for his family to offer visitors *mice on toast*, for lunch, or *crocodile stew*. His father once ate Louis XIV's embalmed heart for dinner.

Dr Buckland boasted that he had eaten everything in the animal kingdom, but the worst thing was mole – that was utterly horrible. He afterwards said that even worse than mole were bluebottles. He was on holiday when a pet leopard died and was buried underneath a flowerbed, so when he came back he dug it up and ate leopard steak.

**Sick-making.** John W. Huton, of Kansas, U.S.A., who had devoured egg-shells, glass, complete bunches of bananas plus their stalks, raw cow's liver, newspapers, catalogues, $11\frac{1}{2}$ dozen eggs at one go and 10 lb. of raw beef – also 1 dozen large lemons without sugar – said the only thing which made him sick was a bag of *cement*.

**Boots.** A Russian called Lomakin in 1904 bet his boots – lost – and ate them.

**Roman gluttons.** Phagon, an official at the court of the Emperor Aurelianus ate a sheep, a pig, 100 loaves of bread and a boar at one sitting.

Arpocras once finished his meal by eating *four tablecloths* and *a broken glass*.

Elagabulos, the Roman Emperor, made his *guests* eat artificial food made of ivory, glass and marble.

**Hand soup.** Customers at a Chinese street stall in Tokyo on 5 July 1978, were served with soup containing parts of the Chinese gang leader Shoichi Murakami. His killers chopped up his hands and put them in the soup to get rid of his fingerprints.

**Invalid food.** When ancient Egyptian children were ill, they were fed *skinned mice*.

**Bicycle.** M. Lotito of France ate a whole bicycle in fifteen days, 17 March to 2 April 1977. He chopped up the tyres and ground the metal parts into iron filings, and for fifteen days he chewed and swallowed. After that he went out for a walk because he had no bicycle to bicycle on.

**Cannibal.** Ex-King Bokassa of the Central African Republic is the most well-known and disliked cannibal. He kept *human steaks* in his fridge.

# MOST DISGUSTING
## AND MOST DELICIOUS FOOD

These two records are the same. Every item in the following list has been named as most delicious *and* most disgusting:

Mud pies, human flesh, flamingo tongues, fried locusts, stinging nettles, rattlesnakes, croctail cocktails, bacon and eggs, semolina, salt porridge, stuffed grasshoppers, termite sausages, butterflies, bees, wasps, dragonflies, fresh lawn-mowings, spinach, hot-dogs, peanut butter, ice-cream, seaweed, dried walrus, caribou stomach, fat lizards, buffalo, acorn bread, camel paw, puppy hams, seal flippers, school dinners, fish and chips, roast chicken, hearts, lights and livers, whale meat-balls, baked worms, sorrel soup, dandelion leaves, sea slugs, bird's-nest soup, cockroaches, cats, dormice, peacocks, frogs' legs, snails, brains, fish eggs, chocolate-coated ants, sardine and toothpaste sandwiches.

*Fill in your most disgusting and your most delicious foods in the Personal Record at the front of this book.*

# DRINK

**Château Piddle.** This rather unusual-sounding drink is an English wine, grown, made and bottled by Peter Dodgson of North Piddle in Worcestershire. Because wine is often called after the place where the grapes are grown, Mr Dodgson asked permission to name his wine after his village. 'No,' they said, 'it's not an accurate description of the contents of the bottle.' (Luckily.) But in February 1979, they said Yes, so now Mr Dodgson's excellent grape-wine is called Château Piddle.

**The foulest drink.** The Japanese liqueur called *Mam* is made from snakes. First of all they mash up venomous snakes called *mamushis*. Then they leave the snakes to ferment in a special liquid. They then pour off the snake juice, bottle it and drink it.

**Coca Cola.** Coca Cola was invented by John S. Pemberton in 1886. It was sold at first as a pick-me-up and brain tonic!

**Cuppas.** A Leeds newsagent holds the world record for drinking cups of tea. He gets up at 5.30 a.m. and drinks eighty-three cups of tea in the day.

**Spiders** do not eat their victims, they *drink* them — covering them with a liquid which makes them dissolve. A tarantula can drink an entire mouse, bones and all, in about a day and a half.

## SWALLOWING

**Frogs.** Mr John McNamara of County Clare swallowed five live frogs in 65 secs. to become the All-Ireland Live-Frog Swallowing Champion. One of his five opponents was disqualified for chewing.

**Minnows.** Professor Daniel Kaiser of St John's College, Minnesota, swallowed 257 live minnows during a lecture on marine biology.

**Snake.** The only snake known to have swallowed a snake is a 9 ft boa constrictor in the London Zoo. This snake and another 8 ft boa both began to eat the same pigeon. The longer snake finished the pigeon, and then kept on swallowing . . .

**Pebbles.** Thomas Gobshill, a 17th-century Englishman, is the world record pebble-swallower. Thomas suffered from wind, and a friend advised him to take a dose of nine round white pebbles a day to cure it. At first it did, but then it didn't, so Thomas increased the dose until he had swallowed 200.

After two and a half years, he was suffering from indigestion, so he called in Sir Charles Hall, famous physician. Sir Charles strapped Thomas upside down to a ladder. The stones came rattling down towards his mouth, but when he stood up again, the stones rattled back into his stomach.

There was no cure for pebbles, so poor Thomas Gobshill suffered from them for the rest of his life.

**Ring.** A diamond ring, worth $35,000 was found inside the stomach of Peter Lazaros of New York on 3 May 1978, after he had died in prison. The ring had disappeared from the Pierre Hotel, New York, a year before.

**Outboard motor.** An outboard motor was swallowed by a crocodile in Australia in 1979.

**Compulsive.** The world's worst compulsive swallower was an American who in 1960 complained of swollen ankles, went into hospital, was operated on and was found to have in his stomach: a 3 lb. piece of metal, 26 keys, 3 sets of rosary beads, 16 religious medals, a bracelet, a necklace, 3 pairs of tweezers, 4 nail clippers, 39 nail files, 3 metal chains, 88 coins and various other items – 258 objects in all.

**Sword.** The longest length of sword swallowed is 27 ins. (69 cm). Alex Linton of Ireland, living in Sarasota, Florida, U.S.A., is the only man to have 'swallowed' four 27-in. blades at one time. He is only 5 ft 3 ins. tall.

**Piranhas.** Piranhas are the animal world's record eaters. Five piranhas can completely devour a horse and its saddle in 5 mins. (The rider would probably take a couple more minutes to chew up.)

**The crocodile** never chews, it swallows. Small stones in its stomach grind up the food.

## THE AMAZING
## HALF-EATEN-APPLE CLUE

A half-eaten Golden Delicious apple set a world record on 11 December 1977. It caught a criminal, all by itself.

Early in the morning of Saturday 3 April 1976, an office building in Southport, Lancashire, was burnt down by an arsonist, causing £28,000 worth of damage.

One room survived, and in that room, police found an apple with a single bite in it. They rushed it immediately (through the Grand National traffic jams) to the home of John Furness in Liverpool. Mr Furness is the world's leading expert on bite marks. He quickly bottled the apple in preserving fluid.

Police picked up Karl Johnson five days later. He lived near by and had a police record for arson. Johnson swore he had been at home at the time, but he agreed to have his teethprints taken. They found his teethprints matched exactly those in the apple – including one unusually round tooth and one slightly jutting forward. He had definitely eaten that apple. He had felt a bit hungry, taken it out of a secretary's drawer while he was ransacking the place and taken one fatal bite. It was the *only clue* that connected Karl Johnson with the crime.

Johnson was tried on 11 December 1977 and convicted – the first man to be convicted on the sole evidence of his teethprints. The odds against two people having identical teeth are, like fingerprints, $2\frac{1}{2}$ billion to 1. You can lie in your teeth, but your teeth can't lie.

## THE WEIRDEST PLACES TO EAT

**Operation Eat-Out.** Cub Scouts were set a challenge in 1979 – to find the weirdest, most way-out places to eat a meal. All over Britain (and even abroad), Cubs ate their meals in the craziest, record-making, completely peculiar and loony places.

Australian Cubs ate in a chauffeur-driven Rolls-Royce in an automatic car-wash.

In Britain, Cubs took their meals in shop windows, with an elephant in Chessington Zoo, in a pig-sty, in a Chieftain Tank, on Concorde 002, upside down on the revolution ride in Blackpool, in a police-dog cage, in the back of a hearse, on a raft in a river.

Ernie Davies the strong-man *supported* twenty-two 1st Cheriton Cubs on a frame for 3 whole minutes while they ate tea.

1st Dursley ate sausage, spaghetti, jelly and cream in the *dentist's chair*.

Orsett Cubs ate on a *sixteen-seater tricycle* cycling round Trafalgar Square.

1st Stoke Golding ate in the back of a *refuse lorry*.

19th Huddersfield had tea in a *pram*.

The Central Folkestone Pack ate kebabs in a *crypt* surrounded by rows of skulls.

Robert Pocock perched with starlings and sparrows on a *bird table*.

Gary Longman had Sunday lunch in the *lavatory*.

1st Stramshall had lunch in a JCB *excavator bucket*; 36th Swansea in a *mincing machine*; 7th Rugby were 70 ft up on a fire service *hydraulic platform*; the Lord Mayor of London ate with 1st Kingshill Otters in a *belfry*; thirty-seven Cubs of the 9th Leicester had soggy sandwiches and watered pop in the *giant bath* of Stoneygate Rugby Club.

Cubs ate sandwiches while *parascending* and 100 ft up in a *balloon* and on the summit of *Snowdon*. 12th Truro tucked into 'tiddy oggies' down Poldark *Mine*. 1st Llanymynech *abseiled down a cliff* to eat a meal on a suspended table.

10th Nelson ate *hot-dogs in kennels*.

Blackpool *exterminated their jelly babies with the Daleks*.

31st Battersea ate on the *Wembley turf*.

AND, bravest of all, 2nd Barton-on-Humber ate their meal at a BROWNIE MEETING.

**Hottest meal.** The British Dangerous Sports Club in 1978 ate their dinner on the side of an erupting volcano. The food kept nice and hot, but the wine got *too* warm.

## THE MISSING RECORD

There are a million records that are *not* in this book.

If there is ONE record that you think, most of all, should be in this book, send it to:

*Puffin Books Ltd*
*536 King's Road*
*London S.W.10 OUH*

Please also put your name, age and address.

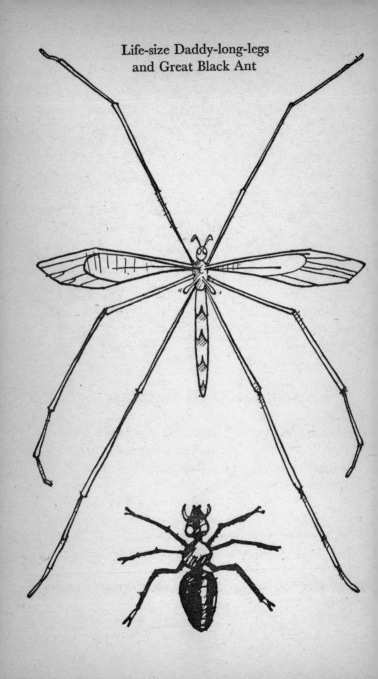

Life-size Daddy-long-legs
and Great Black Ant